SAVING
SALVATION

The Amazing
Evolution
of Grace

STEPHEN SMITH

Foreword by Barbara Cawthorne Crafton

morehouse

HARRISBURG • LONDON

Unless otherwise noted, scripture quotations contained herein are from the New Revised Standard Version Bible, copyright © 1989 by the Division of Christian Education of the National Council of Churches of Christ in the U.S.A. Used by permission. All rights reserved.

Morehouse Publishing, P.O. Box 1321, Harrisburg, PA 17105

Morehouse Publishing, The Tower Building, 11 York Road, London SE1 7NX

Morehouse Publishing is a Continuum imprint.

Printed in the United States of America

Cover design by Laurie Klein Westhafer

Library of Congress Cataloging-in-Publication Data

Smith, Stephen, 1957 Sept. 25-
  Saving salvation : the amazing evolution of grace / Stephen Smith.
    p. cm.
  ISBN 0-8192-2138-4 (pbk.)
  1. Salvation. 2. Salvation—Biblical teaching. 3. Salvation—History of doctrines.
I. Title.
  BT751.3.S63 2005
  234—dc22
                    2004015662

09 08 07 06 05   1 2 3 4 5

This book is dedicated to the glory of God
And to Jan, my wife, whose love and support have enabled me
to do and be far more than I ever dreamed possible.

CONTENTS

ACKNOWLEDGMENTS

There are so many people to thank for helping me write this book. A partial list includes, first, my book reading group. These individuals reviewed chapters as I completed them and then gave their feedback. They certainly played a major role in this work. Thanks to Debra Lynn Hook, the Reverend Allan Belton, Rev. Paul Gaston, Janet Daniels, Pam Zuhl, Rev. John Coil, Dick Smith, Nancy Baxter, Carol Donley, Debbie Shuster, Sarah Adams, John Hopkins, Sarah Koebley, Rev. John Gross, the Very Reverend Tracey Lind, Nancy Sistek, Rev. Masud Syedullah, Rev. Bill Matlack, Reed Stith, Hal Schroeder, Steve Portalupi, Steve Bilsbury, and Russ Wilson. Thanks also to Rev. Barbara Crafton for her support, encouragement, and referrals. Thanks to Rev. Dr. Philip Culbertson and Marcus Borg for their inspiration. Thanks to the churches I have served over the years: St. George's, Dayton, Ohio; Christ Church, Alto, Tennessee; Christ Church, Cincinnati; Redeemer, Lorain, Ohio; Christ Church, Hudson, Ohio; and St. Patrick's, Dublin, Ohio. I can only hope that you learned even half as much from me as I learned from all of you. Thanks go to my parents and grandparents, for the gift of growing up in a home filled with the love of God. I thank my wife, Jan, and my children, Andy and Joy, for their support and love. And finally, I thank God for the love I have so joyfully experienced in this life and for all these wonderful people God sent my way.

FOREWORD

It is some years ago now: a Friday afternoon, busy as usual, full of the interruptions that form the major part of a parish priest's life—our parishes pay us to be interrupted, my friend Philip says, and I think he may have something there. The phone rang and it was for "the pastor"—someone I didn't know, then, and probably someone who wanted money: professional mendicants often call churches late on Friday afternoons.

But it was not a mendicant. It was a young woman, calling from somewhere upstate. She and her partner had moved up there from the Bronx last year, she said, and they had found a church they liked. They loved going to church together: my caller had grown up going to church with the beloved grandmother who raised her, and it meant a lot to her to have church in her new life. The people were friendly and the pastor was friendly. For several months they attended services, made friends, helped out with various projects. They looked forward to Sunday mornings. The pastor was a good preacher, and they liked the music. They could imagine themselves making a permanent spiritual home there, and they wanted a spiritual home.

And so they made an appointment with the pastor to talk with him about joining. They came to his study on the appointed evening, and he received them kindly. He would be delighted to receive them into his congregation, he said. He had a question, though: he knew that they shared an address but had different last names. They were not—how should he put it—living in a lesbian relationship, were they?

Well, yes, we are, one of the women said. Nothing had ever been said, but wasn't it sort of obvious? And people had been so friendly with them, at the church picnic, and at the yardwork day. Nobody had ever questioned them about their living arrangements.

The pastor's demeanor was still kind. In that case, he said with real regret in his voice, I'm afraid I can't accept you as members of our church. You are living in a state of sin. I'm sorry.

The two young women never returned to that church, of course. They were humiliated to think that the people who had been so friendly and kind to them would not have received them at all had they known who they really were. A state of sin, the pastor they so admired had said. It had been hard for each of them, growing up, to come to terms with their sexuality. Other kids had been cruel to each of them in school sometimes, and that cruelty had stung like a lash. It had been hard telling their families; there were still family members who did not know. But at the little country church, it had seemed that an unconditional welcome in Christ had been offered to them unconditionally. But no. There were strings. They were not acceptable to God. Her partner was bitter. Who needs church, anyway, she said angrily. Bunch of hypocrites. But my caller remembered the comfort of her church at home, remembered her grandmother's faith, remembered the white Bible she had been given as a girl, the very one she carried to church now. She remembered safety and love and learning about holiness. And she found our number in the telephone directory and called me late on a Friday afternoon, wanting to know if there was a church that could find the two of them in its understanding of salvation.

I told her a little about the Episcopal Church—hers was Baptist, so the two experiences were very different in some respects. I told her about the sacraments, about the centrality of the Eucharist, about how every baptized person is a member of the Body of Christ and you don't need to do anything more about "joining" than that. I told her about our relationship to the inspired word of God in scripture, how we take it seriously but not always literally. I told her that we valued diversity, that ours was a church in which the love of God is understood to be stronger than the barriers that human beings erect to protect themselves from one another. That we don't think we have all the answers, and that we think that God's will is often a mysterious thing. That was a lot to tell a very young woman in a lot of pain, but she listened with quiet desperation. And then she spoke.

"But—are you saved?"

And I heard in her voice the weight of a thousand sermons about Hell, about the wrath of God. I heard the voices of a thousand good and kind people, convinced that they served a God who decreed a fiery Hell for many, whose invitation into heaven depended primarily on our having a careful and correct belief system and a scrupulous record where certain rules are concerned. I knew that my caller understood being saved to involve a specific moment in which grace came, the hour and minute and second of which was known and remembered, I was saved at 11:17 the morning of April 27 when I accepted Jesus Christ as my Personal Savior, and before that moment I was not saved and would have gone to Hell if I had died.

All of these thoughts took just a moment. She was still waiting for an answer to her question. "But, are you saved?"

And, late on a Friday afternoon, full of sins I knew about and of other sins I had not yet understood, the pastor of a churchful of people who were sinners, too; full, also, of the stunning awareness that the grace of God was flooding my little office at that very moment, shining, pooling its light on the floor, invincible, bigger than any sin I had or anyone else had ever had, lifting everything, I knew the answer. Are you saved? Yes, I told her. Yes, we are.

Barbara Cawthorne Crafton
The Geranium Farm
September 2004

INTRODUCTION

In September 1979, I attended the Episcopal Church's General Convention in Denver, Colorado. It was a time of great change in our church. We formally approved a new prayer book, which translated prayers into modern English, and replaced a much-loved book that only offered Elizabethan references to God as thee and thou. The first women to be ordained in our church had just been elected to serve as deputies to our national convention. Lingering conflicts still persisted over these issues, but I sensed an air of optimism about the future.

As I was leaving Denver, I stopped at a bookstore where I came across *The Emerging Order: God in the Age of Scarcity*, by two social theorists, Jeremy Rifkin and Ted Howard.[1] A new political alliance was forming, the authors said, between conservative evangelical and fundamentalist versions of Christianity and the Republican party—an alliance, the authors predicted, that would determine the future of politics for years to come. I hate to admit it now, but I laughed when I read their theory.

Yet at that time both the conservative evangelicals and the fundamentalist movement—a long way from its discredit in the 1920s during the Scopes "Monkey Trial"—were growing in numbers. And recently created religious television shows such as *The PTL Club,* with Jim and Tammy Faye Bakker, and *The 700 Club,* with Pat Robertson, were hugely popular with millions of viewers. But somehow I just didn't think there were enough of them to affect politics and public policy. After all, I was a member of one of the "mainline denominations," traditional Protestant churches like the Lutheran, Methodist, and Presbyterian, as well as the Roman Catholic Church. We were so arrogant we couldn't imagine any other Christian group having more influence over public life than we did.

I was wrong. Rifkin and Howard were right. Within a year of my visit to that bookstore, an evangelical Christian president, Jimmy Carter, was unseated from office at least partly because his views on public policy issues, more aligned with mainline denominations, were more moderate and liberal than those of the conservative evangelical and fundamentalist Christians. Instead, the conservative Christians threw their support to the Republican party and helped propel Ronald Reagan into the Oval Office. Though Reagan claimed no church affiliation and had a wife who dabbled in astrology, conservatives supported him because his views on issues such as abortion, sexuality, school prayer, and defense against communism matched their own.

It is now a generation later. As I write this introduction, the 2004 presidential race is in full swing, and the topic of gay marriage has grabbed the attention of the nation. But though my own Episcopal church recently consecrated Gene Robinson, its first openly gay bishop—and though many Christians are open to the idea of gay marriage—the media, with its usual broad brush, insists on portraying all Christians as opposed to same-sex relationships. The Episcopal Church may have made a media splash with Robinson's election and consecration, but the public image of Christianity has so shifted in the past twenty-five years that now, whenever Christianity is mentioned, the first reference is always to the views of the more conservative evangelicals and fundamentalists.

The public definition of Christianity has changed. But the change is not just about issues of sexuality. The public understandings of such basic things as our scriptures and the meaning of salvation itself have been altered in the last twenty-five years. The more conservative branches of our faith have defined Christianity for the world around us and have even begun to declare that their brothers and sisters in mainline denominations have, at the very least, perverted the faith, and at the very worst, abandoned it altogether.

Even so, I believe myself to be a person who has experienced the salvation of God. Many times in my life, I have been profoundly aware of God's deep and abiding love for me and for all creation. I have found that love most fully revealed in the person of Jesus of Nazareth, who we Christians call the Christ, the Messiah, the Savior, the Son of God, and God Incarnate. I do my best to be a faithful follower of Jesus, and by doing so I have discovered what Jesus called "abundant life." That experience of God's love as found in Jesus has led me to ordination as a priest in the Episcopal Church.

But I have to admit that I am saddened by the ways in which the public definition of Christianity has changed. What makes me the saddest is that we Christians seem far too ready to declare who is "truly Christian" and who is not. We are far more willing to divide ourselves than to seek any form of unity.

I am also saddened that those of us in the mainline Protestant denominations seem to find ourselves on the defensive. We commiserate with one another about how we don't know our Bible as well as the fundamentalists and conservatives, who challenge us and say we are no longer "truly Christian." I remember one radio/TV preacher in a town I served regularly telling his radio audience to "get out of those dead mainline churches that have lost the faith and come to the place of truth." In response to this kind of criticism, mainline Christians feel inferior. Some even begin to believe we are so wrong that they adopt the views of the fundamentalists but remain in the mainline churches and try to change them from within.

This volume is an attempt to explain the understandings of salvation that I grew up with in the Episcopal Church and have experienced in my own life—and that differ from widely held beliefs in our culture. This is not to say that those beliefs are necessarily wrong. There are problems with the current public understanding of Christianity, but this side of heaven, any human interpretation of the faith will fall short. The problem is, when we stake a claim to the only version of the truth, we tend to paint ourselves into theological corners from which we can never escape. We also deny our history. The meaning of salvation has never been static, but has changed and evolved over time. The current popular definition represents just one manifestation of that evolution.

This book makes the point that no single version of Christianity has a monopoly on the truth. Instead, my hope is that readers will discover the joy of God's salvation no matter what branch they belong to on the Christian family tree. My hope is that—even when they're barraged with the assertions of fundamentalist Christians—they'll know in their hearts the joy of the deeper meaning of God's salvation. And after reading this book, they will not feel defensive when anyone arrogantly dares to claim they are wrong.

CHAPTER 1

DOES SALVATION NEED SAVING?

Grace, the Christian concept of salvation, needs no salvation. It has survived such ungraceful events in Christian history as the Crusades, anti-Jewish pogroms, the violent and forced conversion of indigenous peoples, and even the Church's support of—or blind eye toward—slavery.

But in much of North America, grace no longer sounds like salvation or even like good news. Hellfire and brimstone preaching is alive and well and portrayed in multimedia manifestations. Works righteousness, the idea that we can somehow earn our way to heaven by convincing God how good we are, abounds. And a general sense of confusion surrounds the concepts of grace, salvation, heaven and hell, the kingdom of God, and eternal life. Grace may not need saving, but it could sure use some clarification.

I first encountered confusion about the topic in the year 2000 while teaching a class on the historical Jesus at my parish. A Kent State University professor, Jon Wakelyn, and I reviewed and taught a book called *The Meaning of Jesus: Two Views*, by Marcus Borg and N. T. Wright.[2] When we came to the authors' descriptions of Jesus' preaching of the kingdom of God, we told the class that Jesus and many of his followers probably expected the kingdom of heaven to come on earth. The class reaction startled us. Some claimed to have never heard such a thing. The kingdom was only in the afterlife, they insisted. Jesus came that we might have a personal relationship with him and live a good enough life to get into heaven. Christianity, they asserted, was only about getting into heaven in the next life.

Now Jon and I were startled. There was no mention of the Social Gospel movement that proclaimed the kingdom of God on earth. There was no knowledge of the utopian communities in Christian history that sought to bring about heaven on earth. The emphasis on living "a good enough life" revealed a sense of works righteousness, or the notion that one must earn one's way into heaven.

I began to wonder about the effectiveness of my preaching. In sermons I had supported many of our congregation's outreach efforts by describing them as working toward the kingdom Jesus proclaimed. Now I wondered how that message had been received. Did people want to work for the kingdom or just contribute to a project they hoped would pave their own way to heaven? And what of the Christian Social Gospel movement and civil rights—twentieth-century efforts that sought to combine the Christian desire for the kingdom of God with attempts to promote justice and social welfare (elaborated at greater length in chapter 5)? Clearly most of the members of the class were old enough to remember manifestations of these movements from the 1960s. Did they just lump them in with all the other liberal movements of the 1960s and fail to associate them with the Church and its mission?

As I pressed the class more, I learned that the prevailing attitude about the concepts of grace, salvation, and heaven resembled Marcus Borg's description of his boyhood faith in *The God We Never Knew*:

> In a sentence, the image of Christianity internalized as a child was "Believe now, for the sake of heaven later. . . ." Christianity was about believing in God and Jesus in order to go to heaven.
>
> So fundamental was this notion that if somebody had been able to convince me at age ten or twelve that there was no afterlife, I wouldn't have had any idea why one should be a Christian. It was all about going to heaven.
>
> [This] generated an image of Christianity as a religion of meeting requirements now for the sake of eternal rewards later. There were different opinions about what those requirements were and

whether they were many or few. But requirements there were, and a reward there would be. We were to be judged, whether by a weighing of our deeds, the integrity of our repentance, an assessment of our faith, or some combination; and on that judgment our eternal destiny would depend.[3]

This encounter with the class's minimalist understanding of salvation drove the point home: In our culture, salvation is all about getting your ticket punched on the train ride to the afterlife. It made me start thinking about other occasions when I encountered this minimalism. It was around Halloween, and the newspapers overflowed with ads for one haunted house after another. All of them sought to raise money for charity, from the local Jaycees, to a sports program, to a neighborhood church, but one advertised itself as specifically Christian. I decided to check it out as a possible field trip for my parish youth group. What I found frightened me—not because of the monsters, but because of the message. I was invited to walk with a group down a path that led to the house. Along the way, we passed a depiction of a car accident. Young people hung out the windows of the cars in torn clothes doused with fake blood. One young man—identified by an announcer as a non-Christian—was sprawled over the hood of the car, as if thrown through the windshield. Inside the house, I saw the boy from the hood of the car tormented by devils, demons, slashers, and chainsaw-wielding murderers. The scenes were similar to those from other haunted houses not labeled "Christian." But the message was clear: Become a Christian to avoid the torment of hell when you die.

Counselors stood at the exits, inviting participants to talk about their experiences. I told one of them how disturbed I was by the whole event and pointed out that scaring people into conversion didn't seem an appropriate proclamation of a loving God. Coercion, I insisted, denied the free gift of God's love.

This counselor's only response: "We'll do whatever it takes to bring people to Jesus."

Scaring people into salvation has become widespread. The Christian haunted house has been a part of every community in which I've lived.

Created and staffed by youth ministers and youth groups, such exhibits have had a profound effect on young people, who are often confused and frightened about their future. Even in public high schools, staunch Christian believers frighten fellow students with the prospect of hell if they don't get saved, in a particular way, with a particular message, in relation to a particular church. In every community in which I have lived, I've heard horror stories of "good Christian" high school students harassing their Jewish, Muslim, or Hindu classmates, telling them they need to convert or face damnation. And every year, baccalaureate services for graduating seniors all over the country include some speaker who is trying to convert everyone to Jesus to save them from the fires of hell.

Many of our youth find this message offensive. And they think it is the only message Christianity has to offer. As one young person said to me, "All Christianity is good for is to tell us to do everything we can to get into heaven so we can avoid being fried by a 'loving' God. If that's what it's all about, I don't want anything to do with it." Even young people who are believers struggle when they hear this "get saved or burn in hell" message. Though they go to church, pray regularly, and live good lives, they doubt their own salvation. Their friends tell them they don't believe in the right way. Or they don't believe the truth of the Bible unless they reject Darwin and subscribe to creationism. Or they are told they go to the wrong church. These young people, in the insecurity of youth, become confused and full of doubt. And even when I offer them alternatives, their friends may insist that what I say is heresy—after all, I'm not the right kind of minister from the right kind of church.

This "get saved or burn in hell" attitude has become popular because of a shift in the common understanding of Christianity in North America over the past generation. When I was a child, Christianity was identified with mainline churches, such as Methodist, Presbyterian, and Episcopal. After the election of John F. Kennedy, our first Catholic president, even Roman Catholicism entered the public consciousness as readily identifiable with the public understanding of our faith. At that time, fundamentalism, which requires a literal interpretation of scripture, was viewed as unenlightened, considered marginal, and often associated with a small minority in "the Bible Belt." But since the 1960s, the roles have reversed. The mainline churches have become the marginal Christians, and fundamentalism has become the norm. At the same time, the Christian evangelical movement has grown much more conservative. Evangelicals, by definition, are simply those who preach the good news of Jesus Christ and invite others to follow him. According to that definition, I consider myself an evangelical, too. But a growing number of evangelicals have begun to proclaim a harsh message: that unless believers can point to a day and time when they gave their lives to Jesus, then they're not really Christians at all. Combine this conservative form of evangelicalism with fundamentalism and the result is the hard message, "Get saved or burn in hell."

There are still other minimalist views of salvation with negative effects on our lives. One is the expectation that salvation protects us from all harm. For example, when trouble strikes our lives, we may ask, "Why me?" This is an honest, gut reaction to the pain of life that all pastors deal with. The vast majority of people—pastors included—ask this question at one time or another. But though members of the clergy should be supportive and caring, our response is often complicated by the minimalist view of salvation. More than once I have heard people ask, "Why me? I thought that if I believed in God, and did what was right, my life would always be good." Such a view denies salvation to the martyrs and the missionaries who sacrificed comfortable lives to serve in faraway lands, and it denies all those who suffered for the Gospel either by choice or by force. Scripture and the tradition never said salvation guaranteed an easy life. Yet over and over again I hear this expectation repeated. I know many individuals who couldn't move on in their healing over grief, or loss, or tragedy, until they let go of this expectation.

All of these views of salvation—a ticket to the next world, a way out of the fires of hell, or a guarantee of a pain-free life—fail to capture the depth of what salvation means for Christians. In fact, these views diminish the power of our faith.

Though we need not save the Christian concept of salvation, it may benefit from some clarification. That's what this book is all about. I will examine the history of the concept of salvation in scripture and the traditions of the Church. I will also describe some of the rich ways in which people have encountered the power and presence of God. The Christian church has evolved through the centuries to embrace a rich heritage of interpretation and meaning about how the power of God's love enriches our lives, not just with a heavenly hope, but also even in the here and now. In addition, I will share some of my own stories of how God's love has touched my life.

The current popular understanding of salvation seems so limited to me. But hopefully this short, simple book can offer a wider, richer view of the saving love the God of all creation has for each one of us. This book is a reflection on the depth of the concept of salvation, its roots in scripture, its history, and its application across time. It will also explore where some of the current minimalist ideas and attitudes arose, and look at how they became so popular. But there are other less harsh and judgmental ways to proclaim and preach salvation. In the end, I will attempt to describe new ways to proclaim and preach salvation in order to communicate its depth and power as a manifestation of God's incredible love for us.

CHAPTER 2

~o~

SALVATION IN THE BIBLE: THE HEBREW SCRIPTURES

If you've ever gone head to head with fundamentalists, you probably found out pretty fast that they know their Bible through and through. So you'd assume that their minimalist message of salvation as a guarantee of heaven is grounded in scripture.

It is not. In fact, the Old Testament rarely connects the concepts of salvation and heaven. And a more critical look at the New Testament reveals that Jesus' message of the kingdom of God and eternal life are as much rooted in this life as in the next.

But before looking at what scripture actually says, let's consider the context and history in which our most sacred book came into being.

THE CULTURAL CONTEXT

The place to begin is with the stories of our origin as a people of faith—the Bible. Yet it would be misleading to speak of the "biblical view of salvation," as if there were one concept, one definition that captured all the scriptural references into a single meaning. The Hebrew scriptures came together across many centuries, dating from as long ago as one thousand years before Jesus and reaching their final form about the time of Christ. How do we know this? A simple reading of the introduction to Mark's gospel will reveal a startling discovery. Mark opens with the story of John the Baptist, saying, "As it is written in the prophet Isaiah, 'See, I am sending my messenger ahead of you, who will prepare your way; the voice of one crying in the wilderness: "Prepare the way of the Lord, make his paths straight"'" (Mark 1:2–3).

. There is one problem with Mark's quotation from Isaiah. It isn't all from Isaiah—half the quotation is from the book of the prophet Malachai. How could Mark make such a mistake? Many scholars theorize there may have been divergent forms of the book of Isaiah in the first century C.E. Such a quotation may have been in the version that Mark used—but it just wasn't in the version of the book that finally became standard around the year 70 C.E.

The existence of the Apocrypha offers another clue. The Apocrypha is a set of books written in Greek, telling the story of the Jews' revolt against the Greeks in the second century B.C.E., and of Hanukkah, the rededication of the Temple of Jerusalem after the revolt. The books contain literature describing God's gift of wisdom, such as the book of Ecclesiasticus, and much more.

Many scholars believe that after the Jewish War with Rome (66–70 C.E.), rabbis took refuge in a town in southern Israel called Jamnia, where they made the final decisions on which books would be considered sacred. One decision they made was to exclude the books of the Apocrypha, probably because they were written in Greek rather than Hebrew. Since Christianity was forming at the same time, some Christian groups included the Apocrypha in their sacred texts. And to this day, various Christian denominations debate the importance of such books. Generally, Catholics, Orthodox, and Anglican Christians accept some limited use of the Apocrypha in worship and study, while most Protestants reject it. The existence of the Apocrypha and disagreements about it is evidence that the Old Testament was still coming into formation at the time of Jesus and even after the beginnings of the early Church.

The early Church even debated which books to include in the New Testament well into the middle of the second century. We know this because of a man named Marcion (ca. 150 C.E.), who wanted Christians to acknowledge only the Gospel of Luke, the book of Acts, the authentic letters of Paul, and nothing else. It was Marcion's challenge that led the Church to finally begin declaring, toward the end of the second century, which books it would hold sacred and wh₎ would not.

During all this time of gathering and compiling the scriptures anᴄ deciding on which of them would be known as sacred, the beliefs, attitudes, and understandings about God progressed and changed. What Abraham knew and believed is somewhat different from what the disciples of Jesus knew and believed. Abraham, who lived some two thousand years before Christ, was at the beginning of the Hebrew tradition; the disciples came at the end of the formation of that tradition. So the disciples of Jesus received their faith along with the weight of a tradition and a history that grew and evolved over the years. Abraham had no knowledge of the Exodus, the Ten Commandments, the conquering of the Promised Land, the kingships of David and Solomon, or the Exile of the Jews in Babylon—but Jesus and his disciples did. The faith the disciples received, as outlined in the Old Testament, had gone through many periods of growth, amplification, and clarification over the history of the Hebrew people.

So to say that we could capture all of that biblical thought about the meaning of salvation in a single sentence would be like saying we could describe every era presented at the Metropolitan Museum of Art in New York in just one phrase, or like explaining the rise and fall of the Roman Empire in a sound bite.

Not only was there a growth and progression in the understanding of the faith between the earliest days of the Hebrew people and the time of Jesus, but there has also been a dynamic and changing history of the way people have interpreted and understood those scriptures from the days they were finalized until now. We don't look at the Bible the same way Jesus did. In stark physical reality we can say that Jesus looked at leather or papyrus fragments with Hebrew and Aramaic letters, laboriously written by hand, weathered by age, and wrapped tightly in scrolls. Today we have bound books, easily printed with modern technology, on thin paper with notes and explanations in the margins.

Our physical experience of the Bible is different than that of our spiritual ancestors—the historical background and the expectations we bring when we open it up differ as well. The authors and the early

re didn't know and understand everything we know
)ut the world—that the earth is not at the center of
that germs pass on disease. And they also didn't
..ceptions about salvation. We forget, for example, that
.ase "Saved by grace through faith" was written by Martin
ـuther in the sixteenth century and based on only a single scriptural
reference. Scripture informed Martin Luther's idea of grace, but it was
still his description and interpretation of the books of the Bible that led
him, and the whole Protestant movement, to embrace this concept of
salvation. And perhaps Luther's view was not exactly the same as those
held by the earliest readers of scripture. The first-century readers
where influenced by their own cultural context, including the domi-
nance of the Roman Empire, the marginalization of the poor and pow-
erless, and for many early Christians an expectation that the world
would end in their lifetime. Their view of salvation by grace, through
faith, may have been less personal and psychological than Luther's was.
They may have centered on a hope of being spared during one of
Rome's frequent wars, or being delivered from poverty and degrada-
tion, or even being spared from the early persecutions the Church
experienced in the time of the Roman Empire.

To assume that all our current ways of looking at the world can be
automatically applied to any other time in history, or to a book such as
the Bible that comes to us from history, is called "presentism"—reading the past only in terms of the present. An example can be found in
the way we view a famous figure such as Christopher Columbus.
Today, he comes under criticism for his exploitation and mistreatment
of Native Americans. We forget that Columbus's values and assumptions about how people of different continents might be treated were
not the same as ours today. Rather, back in fifteenth-century Europe,
certain people debated whether or not the Native Americans were even
human. In that context, Columbus's treatment of the natives was
certainly not as unethical as it seems to us today.

An example of how we apply this "presentism" to the Bible is the way
we view the concept of the "truth" of scripture. The popular fundamentalist movement in Christianity proclaims that truth and fact

mean the same thing. Actually, that expectation comes from the last 300 years of scientific revolution in western culture. Yes, facts contain truth. But prior to the scientific and technological revolutions, people understood that truth could come from fiction and story. Good fables, like those of Aesop, could proclaim timeless and honored truths— though everyone knows we can't expect to find factual evidence of a tortoise racing a hare, we recognize that steadily plodding along on a worthwhile project often leads to success. This is truth without a shred of fact in the fable proclaiming it.

But when we open our Bibles, we tend to read with our twenty-first-century bias that truth and fact are synonymous. Though no fundamentalists interpret Jesus' parables as factual, they view almost everything else as such. Unless the Bible itself calls a passage or story an allegory or parable, fundamentalists believe it to be a description of actual factual events—otherwise, they argue, it couldn't be true. This fundamentalist approach has become the dominant, popular way of looking at scripture in our day. We forget that this view is based on the notion that truth and fact are synonymous, an idea that has only been a part of western culture since the seventeenth century (I will discuss this in greater detail in chapter 6).

Just suppose we applied the concept of presentism to the book of Jonah, transforming it from an allegory to journalism. We'd assume that disputing the fact of Jonah being swallowed by a great fish would endanger the *truth* of the story. Yet, even if it never happened that way, the book of Jonah still conveys an important truth in an allegorical way. It shows us how far from God we roam when we don't love our enemies the way God loves them. It shows us that, in the end, God defends his love for even those we would rather hate. The biblical authors wanted to convey this truth, and we complicate and diminish it when we insist that the story conform to our modern understanding of truth as fact. Instead of teaching us to love our enemies, the book of Jonah becomes an opportunity to argue over whether or not a giant fish could really swallow a human being.

Yet the reality is that we look at the Bible through twenty-first-century eyes, staring across time and through the cultural and language revolutions of the last twenty centuries, back to a set of books that came into final form almost two thousand years ago. We often read the books of the Bible with the mindset of presentism, as if they were written yesterday, in the midst of our own culture, with all of our current understandings of the world. We forget that the Bible has gone through at least three major language translations (from Greek and Hebrew, to Latin, and then to English for the British and North Americans). We forget that the Bible has spanned complete changes in culture, from the Hebrew world, to the Greek, to the Roman, to the Middle Ages, to the rise of the European empires, and finally to the democratic, scientific, industrial, and technological revolutions of the last 300 years.

Though we consider the Bible a timeless book, and the primary source for our understanding of ourselves as the people of God, it came into being in a time and place different from our own. Biblical scholars use other ancient texts, archaeological evidence, and studies in ancient languages and cultures to try and make sense of that world. In their scholarship they try to recreate the world in which the Bible came into being, in hopes that we will understand it better.

Though it may seem arrogant to think we can recreate a worldview or understanding so far removed from our own, scholars try nevertheless. And their insights can give us an appreciation for meaning in the biblical text that we may not get at our first reading, or may never have heard before, even about such a basic concept in our faith as salvation.

SALVATION AS RESCUE

Looking at the Old Testament in its context, we can find many meanings applied to the concept of salvation. In fact, the very word *salvation* in Hebrew, *Yeshu,* is the same root word for the names Joshua and Jesus—the saviors. So salvation is not just an idea about God's relationship with us, but a name for those who help us to understand that relationship. But it is the Exodus, that time when the Hebrew slaves escaped their overlords in Egypt and passed through the Red Sea, that may provide the oldest reference to *Yeshu.*

Many scholars believe that the Song of Miriam (Exodus 15:21), attributed to Moses' sister and sung after the deliverance at the Red Sea, is the oldest Hebrew writing in the Old Testament.[4] The Hebrew in this passage is very simple and straightforward, giving a summary of the defining event in Israel's history: "Sing to the Lord, for he has triumphed gloriously; horse and rider he has thrown into the sea."

Preceding this simple song in the book of Exodus is a later piece called the Song of Moses. It begins with almost the same words as Miriam's short song, but then the next line states, "The Lord is my strength and my might, and he has become my *Yeshu* [salvation]" (Exodus 15:2).

Here may be one of the oldest references in scripture to the word *salvation*. In its context it has nothing to do with our modern obsession with seeing salvation almost exclusively in terms of the next life. Instead, it is all about this life. The people of Israel have been rescued from a pursuing army by means so marvelous (the parting of the sea) that the Israelites attribute their triumph to God. This rescue itself is called salvation. Here we have a very clear picture of the earliest biblical understanding of salvation. It is God's people receiving God's help in a time of need.

This early biblical reference to the concept of salvation clearly gives little or no support to the idea of salvation as something *only* otherworldly. Even so, later generations used the Red Sea account to interpret personal salvation. Jesus' Last Supper, which later became the basis for the Christian ritual of communion, is seen as the new Passover (Passover being the Jewish ritual remembrance of the Red Sea experience and all that led up to it, including the deliverance from the final plague and the flight from Egypt). Paul states that "Christ our Passover is sacrificed for us," to describe the salvation Christians experience in following Jesus. Some hymn writers referred to otherworldly and heavenly salvation with metaphors like crossing the Red Sea, or being rescued from death as if from a pursuing enemy. For example, the Easter hymn "Come, Ye Faithful Raise the Strain" borrows liberally from the Red Sea metaphor. The hymn, in total, highlights Jesus' resurrection and the Christian hope for a life to come. But one verse refers exclusively to the Red Sea salvation:

Come, ye faithful raise the strain
of triumphant Gladness!
God hath brought his Israel into joy from sadness:

loosed from Pharaoh's bitter yoke
Jacob's sons and daughters,
led them with unmoistened foot
through the Red Sea Waters.

(The Hymnal 1982, 200)

Thus, singing this hymn on Easter morning connects the ancient salvation event of rescue at the Red Sea with the longed-for salvation of life to come through Jesus' resurrection.

These references, however, are all later adaptations using the Red Sea account as the starting point for a metaphor. The starting point itself, the account of the Exodus, is about this life and seeing the power of God aiding *God's people* to escape from oppression and possible annihilation.

I emphasize "God's people" because clearly this salvation happens to everyone in the group following along with Moses. There is no distinction between good or bad, moral or immoral. God saves all of "Jacob's sons and daughters," all the children of Abraham, simply because they are children of Abraham—God's people. In our individualistic age, we tend to think of salvation in very personal terms, with people asking, "Are you [singular] saved?" or "Do you have a personal relationship with Jesus Christ?" In the Exodus account, we are told nothing about the state of any individuals, except perhaps for Moses. God saves an entire people by this mighty act.

Though the otherworldly view gets little support from this particular use of the word *salvation* in the Red Sea account, the modern view that considers salvation as a kind of personal protection from harm in this life could easily fixate on this story. From this perspective, one could say, "See! God rescued his people when they were at the Red Sea waters; why can't he rescue me from my cancer?"

It is a legitimate question. But it is a question that does not take into account the fullness of what we might call Israel's salvation story. Though God rescued the Israelites at the Red Sea, there were many other events from which God did not shield the people. For example, despite the warnings of the prophet Jeremiah, in the year 586 B.C.E., Nebuchadnezzar sacked the city of Jerusalem and carried off the leadership into exile. Yet, what the people of Israel, across the ages, began to realize was that salvation as expressed in this one event in history we call the Exodus did not guarantee salvation from all other disastrous events. The Red Sea confirmed that the people of Israel were the chosen ones, but only as manifested across many generations, not in protection from each and every possible event of evil, for each and every individual. The Israelites, in essence, used the account of deliverance at the Red Sea to develop one of their views of salvation: the long-term view. Perhaps being the chosen people did not protect them from all harm, but over time, their "salvation" would be manifest in the real events of this life.

One of the best modern examples of applying this biblical understanding of long-term salvation can be found in two scenes from the musical *Fiddler on the Roof*. In one scene, the main character, Tevya, reflecting on the persecution of the Jews in Russia, says, "Lord, I know we are the chosen people. But couldn't you choose someone else for a change?" In this way, he points out that being chosen does not always mean being protected from all harm. And at the end of the musical, as Tevya and his fellow Jews leave their hometown because of persecution, the rabbi's son asks, "We have waited our whole lives for the Messiah. Wouldn't this be a good time for him to come?" To which the rabbi responds, "We will just have to wait for him somewhere else."

Here is manifest the long-term view of salvation found in Judaism. Not once do the characters deny their salvation, their sense of being chosen by God, simply because things are going badly at the moment. They are still the chosen ones, even if they have to wait for the fullest manifestation of what this may mean. Just so, those of us who know God, who know salvation, may not always find ourselves shielded from the pain of life. However, as with the Israelites, over the long term—the span of a lifetime or the span of generations—we see the power of God's salvation in the course of human events in this life.

If we look at the entire Old Testament, we can see that this idea of God choosing Israel seems to be the primary view of salvation. Salvation, being saved, meant the realization that one was part of God's elect. Individual events of salvation, deliverance at the Red Sea, or personal deliverance from tragedy were only seen as manifestations of this greater salvation.

THE HEBREW HEAVENLY HOPE

What is conspicuously absent from the Old Testament view of salvation is much of a connection with heaven, hell, or the afterlife. In fact, the Hebrew scriptures contain very few references to any of these concepts. The references to any kind of afterlife are so few, in fact, that by the time of Jesus, one Jewish sect, the Sadducees, still did not acknowledge an afterlife. The Sadducees believed that this life was all there was, and it was only in this life that salvation was experienced. Though we call the Sadducees a sect, they weren't some small, out-of-the-way, unheard-of group. In fact, they controlled the mainstream of Judaism in Jesus' day. They even controlled the office of the High Priest; Caiaphas, the High Priest of the Temple, before whom Jesus appeared the night before his crucifixion, was a Sadducee.

When we look at the biblical evidence, it is no wonder that a group uncertain of the afterlife could exist all the way into Jesus' day. The few references to an afterlife that appear in the Old Testament are dissimilar from one another. What follows is a brief collection of biblical images concerning life after death. This is by no means an exhaustive compilation or analysis, but simply enough to give a sense of how the Hebrew scriptures deal with this topic.

One of the most vivid afterlife images in the Old Testament comes from the story of kings David and Saul. Saul was the first king of Israel, and his story has an ignoble end. In 1 Samuel 28, Saul is about to enter the final battle of his life. He is worried about the outcome and anxious that David covets his throne. Abandoned by his advisor, Samuel, who died shortly afterward, King Saul desperately seeks out a medium to conjure up the spirits of the dead.

It's interesting that Saul has outlawed mediums and such practices as divining. When this story was recorded, were the dead to be left alone, not thought of, not contacted or considered in any way to be alive? We don't know. But the fact that Saul has outlawed such practices as seeking to speak with or contact the dead may hint that they were considered in some way foul or spiritually unclean. It's also interesting that although Saul has banned all mediums from the land, the soldiers immediately know where to find one. Like prostitution, the state can pass laws but cannot stop the process. What follows is a brief selection from the account.

Now Samuel had died, and all Israel had mourned for him and buried him in Ramah, his own city. Saul had expelled the mediums and the wizards from the land. The Philistines assembled, and came and encamped at Shunem. Saul gathered all Israel, and they encamped at Gilboa. When Saul saw the army of the Philistines, he was afraid, and his heart trembled greatly. When Saul inquired of the Lord, the Lord did not answer him, not by dreams, or by Urim, or by prophets. Then Saul said to his servants, "Seek out for me a woman who is a medium, so that I may go to her and inquire of her." His servants said to him, "There is a medium at Endor."

So Saul disguised himself and put on other clothes and went there, he and two men with him. They came to the woman by night. And he said, "Consult a spirit for me, and bring up for me the one whom I name to you." The woman said to him, "Surely you know what Saul has done, how he has cut off the mediums and the wizards from the land. Why then are you laying a snare for my life to bring about my death?" But Saul swore to her by the Lord, "As the Lord lives, no punishment shall come upon you for this thing." Then the woman said, "Whom shall I bring up for you?" He answered, "Bring up Samuel for me." When the woman saw Samuel, she cried out with a loud voice; and the woman said to Saul, "Why have you deceived me? You are Saul!" The king said to her, "Have no fear; what do you see?" The woman said to Saul, "I see a divine being coming up out of the ground." He said to her, "What is

his appearance?" She said, "An old man is coming up; he is wrapped in a robe." So Saul knew that it was Samuel, and he bowed with
his face to the ground, and did obeisance (1 Samuel 28:3–14).

King Saul succeeds in bringing forth the spirit of Samuel, but what
does he get? Samuel is a shade of himself and later complains of his rest
being disturbed.

The Jews, at least at the point when this story was compiled for the
Hebrew scriptures, seemed to believe in the afterlife simply as a hold-
ing place called Sheol, where one rested after this life was over. Little
different than the Greek concept of Hades, Sheol is the place where the
dead go—and where they experience neither bliss nor punishment,
but simply existence. Mentions of Sheol in the Hebrew scriptures paint
a grim picture:

> *Sheol* cannot thank thee, death cannot praise thee;
> those who go down to the pit cannot hope for thy
> faithfulness. (Isaiah 38:18)

> The dead are miserable, insubstantial shades, and it is
> better to be a living dog than a dead lion.
> (Ecclesiastes 9:4)

Perhaps this view of the afterlife was influenced by the Greek concept
of the three-tiered universe. The concept looked something like this:

HEAVEN

The place of the gods (or God and angels), where all
true power was to be found. All earthly events were
ultimately determined here.

EARTH

The land of mortals, who lived out the will
of God(s)

HADES (Sheol)
The place of the dead, the place of the immortal soul

One cannot overemphasize how much this Greek tradition influenced the final version of the Old Testament and eventually the New. After all, the Greeks, under Alexander, conquered the known world in the fourth century B.C.E. Convinced of the superiority of their philosophies and religion, they exported them to every conquered nation. Even Rome, when it conquered Greece, simply borrowed many of its best ideas. By the time of Jesus, Greek was the preferred language of the Mediterranean world. The power of Greek culture throughout the known world—like that of present-day American culture—influenced everything and everyone. And as Greek concepts influenced the Hebrew and Christian traditions, both religions began to hint at the Greek concept of the immortality of the soul through the concept of Sheol. In fact, the philosophical idea of Jesus' Ascension owes much of its origin to this Greek view of the universe. The Greeks believed that those truly in control of the universe were in heaven, so the Christians explained that Jesus had to ascend to the heavens to be truly understood as "lord of all."

But even prior to the Greek conquest, some Jewish ideas had begun to emerge linking salvation with hope for life to come. Take for example, Ezekiel's prophecy to the dry bones, within the context of the Jewish exile in Babylon (586–536 B.C.E.). Ezekiel, trying to convince the Jews in exile that they still have hope, is granted by God a vision to help him and the people appreciate that hope:

> The hand of the Lord came upon me, and he brought me out by the spirit of the Lord and set me down in the middle of a valley; it was full of bones. He led me all around them; there were very many lying in the valley, and they were very dry. He said to me, "Mortal, can these bones live?" I answered, "O Lord God, you know." Then he said to me, "Prophesy to these bones, and say to them: O dry bones, hear the word of the Lord. Thus says the Lord God to these bones: I will cause breath to enter you, and you shall

live. I will lay sinews on you, and will cause flesh to come upon you, and cover you with skin, and put breath in you, and you shall live; and you shall know that I am the Lord." (Ezekiel 37:1–6)

This story, told in the context of a vision, may be an allegory telling the Jews that even in exile, even as a defeated army left dead in a valley, they will yet revive: They may be down, but they are not out. New life will come, even if it seems as miraculous and impossible as skin grafting onto bones and breath filling lifeless bodies. This story is consistent with the idea of salvation as God's election. The Jews saw God's election as having redeeming value across time. Even when things were bad, as they were during the Babylonian captivity, the Jews trusted that as God's chosen people they would be vindicated in this life. And this vindication was viewed as the very meaning of salvation.

But add this prophetic image of new life animating dead bones to the Greek concept of the immortality of the soul and suddenly the Jews come to develop an idea unique to them: the resurrection of the body.

This is more than the immortality of the soul. For one thing, the Jews didn't settle for either Hades or Sheol being simply places for the dead. To them, God, who is everywhere, cannot be absent even from the place of the dead.

If I ascend to heaven, you are there; if I make my bed in Sheol, you are there . . . even there your hand shall lead me, and your right hand shall hold me fast. (Psalm 139:8–10)

In fact, one Hebrew image from the Apocrypha, written after the Greek conquest, even points to the idea of the immortal soul resting not in Sheol, but in a kind of peace in the very hands of God:

But the souls of the righteous are in the hand of God,
and no torment will ever touch them.
In the eyes of the foolish they seemed to have died,
and their departure was thought to be a disaster,

and their going from us to be their destruction;

but they are at peace.

For though in the sight of others they were punished, their hope
is full of immortality.

(Wisdom of Solomon 3:1–4)

This verse also contains the beginnings of the idea that only "the righteous" will enjoy any peace in the next life.

But Judaism—a religion rooted in things of the earth—wasn't entirely
comfortable with the Greek idea of the immortality of the soul. Adam,
after all, was created from the mud, and salvation was revealed through
action (the parting of the Red Sea) and the giving of a physical thing
(the Promised Land). Salvation was embodied in people—Abraham,
Isaac, and Jacob—and human events—the return from exile. The
immortality of the soul was just too ethereal for Jewish theology. It
wasn't until the book of Job, probably assembled after the Greek conquest, that images of the immortal soul are joined with the idea of new
life coming even to dead skin and bones. Job sums up the concept of
the resurrection of the body in its briefest and most succinct:

For I know that my Redeemer lives,

and that at the last he will stand upon the earth;

and after my *skin* has been thus destroyed,

then in my *flesh* I shall see God,

whom I shall see on my side,

and my eyes shall behold, and not another.

(Job 19:25–27, italics mine)

The resurrection of the body, though it owes some of its origin to the
Greek idea of the immortal soul, is in the end a thoroughly Jewish idea.
It refers to a *bodily* existence after this life. It does not deny death or

envision an immortal soul that exists apart from the body. After all, God creates us in a mortal life, with a definite beginning and end. At the end we go to the place of the dead, or Sheol. And it is only by the gift of God that we are given new life, new "bodily" existence in an afterlife or heaven. Paul, in his letter to the Corinthians, amplifies this Hebrew concept when he says that the resurrected body comes about in a way not unlike a new plant growing from a seed. One dies (our mortal selves) in order that another thing may be born (the resurrected body) (1 Corinthians 15).

By the time of Jesus, a movement had developed in Judaism that foresaw a life after this one, in which we would receive new heavenly bodies. The Pharisees became the primary proponents of this concept. But they didn't call this hope for the resurrection "salvation." Rather, to them the afterlife was an extension of the salvation already granted the people of Israel by reason of their election.

The Jewish Story of Salvation

Reading through the entire Hebrew Bible shows that the people of God have experienced salvation in many ways. Called into being by the summons of Abraham and surviving the barrenness of Sarah, the near sacrifice of Isaac, the feuding of Jacob and Esau, the slavery in Egypt, wanderings in the wilderness, war with the Philistines, and even exile in Babylon, they found salvation in being the chosen people who could survive through all calamities, shepherded by God and embraced as God's people. Even the beginnings of an idea of life after death, of salvation in the next life, have their roots in the idea of salvation as realized in this life, in the reality of human history.

CHAPTER 3

SALVATION IN THE BIBLE: THE NEW TESTAMENT

Understanding the Christian scripture's view of salvation must begin with the main character of our Christian story: Jesus. Though the Gospels portray him as constantly fighting with the Pharisees, he had a lot in common with them. Like them he was a teacher and interpreter of the meaning and application of the Law of Moses, and a believer in resurrection from the dead. From the resurrection accounts themselves, to John's account of the raising of Lazarus, it seems obvious that Jesus and his early followers were proponents of this idea of the resurrection of the body. But was this otherworldly concept at the heart of Jesus' understanding of salvation? Was everything Jesus taught simply about what it takes to get to the resurrection, to get into heaven? Hardly.

Salvation is the central theme of the Gospels, the book of Acts, and the letters of Paul. But its meaning is far more complex than simply a recipe for getting into heaven. The Danish theologian Edward Schillebecckx counts no fewer than thirteen different ways in which the New Testament describes salvation.[5] For the sake of this work, I will concentrate on three: the idea of the kingdom, eternal life, and the cross of Jesus.

THE KINGDOM IS HERE AND NOW

Entire books have been written about Jesus' and the early Church's understanding of the kingdom, and there is no way to summarize them all here. Instead, let's look at two features of the kingdom: its roots in the Hebrew scriptures' concept of salvation and its connection with the here and now.

The primary meaning of salvation in the Hebrew scriptures is membership in the people of God, God's chosen. The salvation of the elect is worked out over the course of history, across generations. God's people may have their ups and downs, but God will always vindicate them eventually. They may be enslaved, but they will return home one day; they may be oppressed, but the oppressors will always be defeated. Salvation will be realized in this life by recurring vindication of the people of God.

By the time of Jesus, an expectation had grown that Israel's salvation would be revealed through a new kind of kingdom. A group called the Zealots, who resented the Roman occupation of Israel, expected the rise of a great king like David, whereas others like the Essenes, the community that produced the Dead Sea Scrolls, thought the times were too corrupt for a temporal king. The latter hoped instead for a day when God alone would be king, as in the days before Saul, David, and Solomon. They pictured a time like the one described in the book of Judges, when God appointed charismatic leaders to guide his people through crises.

During this time, Israel considered itself under God's direct rule. If a leader was needed, then God would raise one, called a judge, for the time. The judges saw themselves as selected by God for a specific purpose: to respond to the precise situation or threat faced by God's people. Judges offered leadership in countering these threats and then disappeared into obscurity again. Because these leaders were called by God, and because they did not behave like kings—building royal cities and passing on power to their children—the Israelites considered God to be their true ruler. This form of government, with God as the ultimate leader, is called a theocracy.

It is clear from the biblical evidence—especially the parable of the trees from Judges 9—that the Jews idealized theocracy over all other forms of government. Gideon (Jerubbaal), one of the judges, responded to an attack by the Midianites and drifted back into obscurity once the crisis was over. His son Abimelech, however, seeking the throne for himself, killed all his brothers but Jotham and proclaimed himself as king. Jotham compared the idea of replacing the kingship of God with the kingship of a man to something as silly as making the bramble bush the king of the trees.

Now Abimelech son of Jerubbaal went to Shechem to his mother's kinsfolk and said to them and to the whole clan of his mother's family, "Say in the hearing of all the lords of Shechem, 'Which is better for you, that all seventy of the sons of Jerubbaal rule over you, or that one rule over you?' Remember also that I am your bone and your flesh." So his mother's kinsfolk spoke all these words on his behalf in the hearing of all the lords of Shechem; and their hearts inclined to follow Abimelech, for they said, "He is our brother." They gave him seventy pieces of silver out of the temple of Baal-berith with which Abimelech hired worthless and reckless fellows, who followed him. He went to his father's house at Ophrah, and killed his brothers the sons of Jerubbaal, seventy men, on one stone; but Jotham, the youngest son of Jerubbaal, survived, for he hid himself. Then all the lords of Shechem and all Beth-millo came together, and they went and made Abimelech king, by the oak of the pillar at Shechem.

When it was told to Jotham, he went and stood on the top of Mount Gerizim, and cried aloud and said to them, "Listen to me, you lords of Shechem, so that God may listen to you. The trees once went out to anoint a king over themselves. So they said to the olive tree, 'Reign over us.' The olive tree answered them, 'Shall I stop producing my rich oil by which gods and mortals are honored, and go to sway over the trees?' Then the trees said to the fig tree, 'You come and reign over us.' But the fig tree answered them, 'Shall I stop producing my sweetness and my delicious fruit, and go to sway over the trees?' Then the trees said to the vine, 'You come and reign over us.' But the vine said to them, 'Shall I stop producing my wine that cheers gods and mortals, and go to sway over the trees?' So all the trees said to the bramble, 'You come and reign over us.' And the bramble said to the trees, 'If in good faith you are anointing me king over you, then come and take refuge in my shade; but if not, let fire come out of the bramble and devour the cedars of Lebanon.'" (Judges 9:1–15)

Jotham's scathing parable led to the rejection of Abimelech, but eventually the people prevailed and asked for a king. They complained to the judge Samuel (1 Samuel 8) that he was old and could not continue to lead them. They wanted a king. Although Samuel tried to dissuade them, he eventually relented, only because he was instructed by God to do so: "It is not you they have rejected, but me" (1 Samuel 8:7). Clearly, this call for a king meant the people had given up on the idea of theocracy.

Only four kings in the history of Israel have had anything good said about them: David, Solomon, Uzziah, and Josiah. Most of the rest are described by the epitaph repeated over and over again in 1 and 2 Kings, "And [fill in the name of the king] did what was evil in the sight of the Lord."

By Jesus' day, kings—or any leaders other than God—were still regarded with suspicion. The Maccabees, though they led a successful revolt against Greek overlords (ca. 175 B.C.E.), could not govern a nation. Herod, though he called himself "The Great," was nothing more than a Roman puppet. Some even viewed the temple leadership as corrupt. The Essenes lived in self-imposed exile in the desert near the Dead Sea at least partly because of their negative view of the temple leadership in Jerusalem. This monastic sect felt that the Sadducees, who controlled the temple, made too many concessions to the Romans, and so they retreated to the desert to await God's restoration of purity to their holy place.

Into this history of bad kings and corrupt leaders arose the theology of the kingdom of God. It was a complex and varied set of views collected under one basic premise: God is ultimately in charge and this would be revealed in this life, in something called the kingdom of God, the reign of God, or the kingdom of heaven.

The most extreme view in this theology was the apocalyptic one. This held that the current state of affairs was so horrible that it could only be remedied by a cosmic battle between good and evil, in which God would be revealed as final victor, to establish a kingdom if not on earth then in a future heavenly realm. There were various interpretations naming the evil parties to be destroyed by God: from Rome, to corrupt Jewish leaders, to Satan. But whoever they might be, their destruction was assured, and victory would belong to God. Much of this thought made its way into the New Testament in the Revelation to John. As a result, the language in this book became the source for many of the images we ascribe to our hope for heaven.

Another kingdom-of-God view assumed that a king like David would rise to power, throw off the oppression of Rome, and restore the people of God as a nation. Though he would be king, he would be so close to God that it would be clear that God was fully in charge. This was the view of the Zealots.

Though Jesus did have some apocalyptic notions about the kingdom, he seemed to have a view unique to himself. He saw the reign of God as something available right now, though it might be mysterious, hidden, and found in unexpected ways and places. It is like finding a pearl of great price, he said, or a treasure hidden in a field; it is like the last turning out to be first. This is a very Jewish concept, if we consider the stories of David, Jacob, Joseph, and of Israel itself. David, Jesse's youngest son, turns out to be the best king. Jacob, the younger brother, carries on the promises to Abraham. Joseph, the brother sold into slavery, becomes powerful in Egypt and eventually rescues his family. And the little nation of Israel proclaims itself the chosen people of the God of all creation. The last always seem to be first in the Old Testament, which of course was the Bible of Jesus and his contemporaries. What's more, the kingdom of God is like a seed planted in the ground that yields more fruit than anyone could ever expect, or like a hated Samaritan helping a half-dead Jew lying by the side of the road. It is a wedding banquet or feast that everyone gets to attend, and where the wine never runs out. It is the runaway coming home to acceptance and love, rather than cruelty and rejection.

All of Jesus' images and parables about the kingdom of God use everyday images from the lives of the people. Who in Jesus' day would not have understood about planting seed, and the joy of incredible yields? Who didn't know of the Jews' hatred of the Samaritans? Who wouldn't have dreamed of finding something unexpected out in the fields, a treasure whose value would make plowing unnecessary? Who didn't know about weddings, feasts, and homecomings?

What Jesus is telling the people in his parables and stories is that the reign of God can be found in the events of everyday life. In our attitude, our approach to the world, and our relationship with God, we can discover the power of God's reign. God is ultimately in charge, despite appearances to the contrary, and to realize that, all we need to do is look around.

Looking around, first-century Jews could see Rome and all its power. They could see the corruption of the leadership in Jerusalem. They could see a world filled with pain, toil, and drudgery. But in the first century, they might also have seen or heard of a teacher and healer named Jesus of Nazareth. He had feasts with outcasts. He went to weddings and celebrated. He healed those who were sick. He cared for the lowly and ordinary, and in so doing proclaimed that the kingdom of God was at hand, in the midst of everyone around him.

The painful circumstances of their lives may not have changed. But Jesus came and announced that God was in charge anyway, right here and right now, although it might not look that way. This is what Matthew, Mark, and Luke were pointing to when they used the phrases "kingdom of God" and "kingdom of heaven" in their accounts.

ETERNAL LIFE IN THE PRESENT TENSE: JOHN'S GOSPEL

The exception to this kingdom theology is the Gospel of John, where the phrase "kingdom of God" rarely appears. Instead, John uses the expression "eternal life" to describe a similar idea. You might assume the words "eternal life" refer only to the next life rather than to the reign of God right here and now. Eternal life, after all, is what we hope for when we die. But John uses this phrase in a much more "this-worldly" sense. To understand John's meaning, let us consider the tenses of the verbs in the Gospel of John's description of Jesus' encounter with Nicodemus.

Now there was a Pharisee named Nicodemus, a leader of the Jews. He came to Jesus by night and said to him, "Rabbi, we know that you are a teacher who has come from God; for no one can do these signs that you do apart from the presence of God." Jesus answered him, "Very truly, I tell you, no one can see the kingdom of God without being born from above." Nicodemus said to him, "How can anyone be born after having grown old? Can one enter a second time into the mother's womb and be born?" Jesus answered, "Very truly, I tell you, no one can enter the kingdom of God without being born of water and Spirit. What is born of the flesh is flesh, and what is born of the Spirit is spirit. Do not be astonished that I said to you, 'You must be born from above.' The wind blows where it chooses, and you hear the sound of it, but you do not know where it comes from or where it goes. So it is with everyone who is born of the Spirit." Nicodemus said to him, "How can these things be?" Jesus answered him, "Are you a teacher of Israel, and yet you do not understand these things? Very truly, I tell you, we speak of what we know and testify to what we have seen; yet you do not receive our testimony. If I have told you about earthly things and you do not believe, how can you believe if I tell you about heavenly things? No one has ascended into heaven except the one who descended from heaven, the Son of Man. And just as Moses lifted up the serpent in the wilderness, so must the Son of Man be lifted up, that whoever believes in him may have eternal life.

"For God so loved the world that he gave his only Son, so that everyone who believes in him may not perish but *may have* eternal life.

"Indeed, God did not send the Son into the world to condemn the world, but in order that the world might be saved through him. Those who believe in him are not condemned; but those who do not believe are condemned already, because they have not believed in the name of the only Son of God. (John 3:1–18, italics mine)

From this point forward in John's gospel, whenever the phrase "eternal life" appears, it is spoken of in the present tense. The gospel writer uses the phrase "kingdom of God" just once to connect what he is talking about with the people who already know Matthew, Mark, and Luke (after all, John's gospel was written after those three). Then, he introduces a new phrase, "eternal life," but always as a present tense reality from this point forward in the gospel.

> Whoever believes in the Son *has* eternal life (John 3:36, italics mine)

> Those who eat my flesh and drink my blood *have* eternal life (John 6:54, italics mine)

There are more than a dozen such references, all using the present tense. John's gospel is telling us, over and over again, that to know Jesus, to believe in Jesus, to follow Jesus, to take part in the Eucharist, are actions that all constitute eternal life here and now. As a priest in the Episcopal Church, one of the phrases I can use to administer communion hearkens to this concept: "The Body and Blood of our Lord Jesus Christ *keep* you in everlasting life" (Book of Common Prayer, 361). It is not "give you," or "assure you of a future life," but rather "keep you" in what you already possess.

A twentieth-century English theologian named C. H. Dodd noticed this emphasis in John's gospel on the present possession of eternal life and developed a theology called "Realized Eschatology."[6] In essence, it states that Jesus, through his life, death, and resurrection, and through our relationship with him, has already given us a foretaste of the realities of heaven. In some way, heaven, eternal life, is already here. Dodd had to modify that theology substantially in light of both world wars and the Holocaust. After all, the world didn't look much like heaven on earth. He came up with the idea of eternal life being "here, but not yet fully realized."

What I find most interesting about the Nicodemus encounter is that these verses from the Gospel of John are the ones most often quoted by preachers and evangelists concentrating on a strictly otherworldly view of salvation. In fact, anyone who watches football on TV has seen a reference to Nicodemus's night visit with Jesus. It is painted on bedsheets and held up behind goalposts whenever there is an extra point or field goal attempt. Huge, spray-painted letters declare JOHN 3:3 or JOHN 3:16. John 3:3 refers to the phrase, "born from above" (NRSV) or "born again" (KJV). John 3:16 says "For God so loved the world that he gave his only Son, so that everyone who believes in him may not perish but may have eternal life."

Often those who focus on these passages in sermons speak only about the next life: believe now for the sake of heaven later; be transformed, born again, or from above now to receive heaven later. But a simple reading of the tense of the verbs, and a reference to a scholar such as C. H. Dodd, lets us know that believing now, being transformed now, means that we are already experiencing eternal life.

THE TRUE BELIEVER

Belief, like salvation, is another term that has suffered because of the minimalist nature of our culture. Belief has come to mean little more than assent to an idea, concept, or fact as valid or true. Such a minimal meaning really has almost no meaning at all. When I was a high school student and the subject of religion would come up around the lunch table, invariably the discussion would turn to what it really takes to get into heaven. Someone would cite John 3:16, and then we would ask one another: What does it really mean to believe in God? If we just say I believe that God exists, is that enough? Is that all it takes to receive eternal life? Our discussions assumed that John's gospel implied a future reward, not a current one.

Eventually, someone would counter that simply believing isn't enough—you have to be good, too. But how good do you actually have to be? Before we knew it, we'd left behind the question of belief and the minimalist interpretation we'd given it, and moved on to a discussion of morality—not necessarily a bad way to go, but in the end we'd given little more than lip service to either topic.

I came across this argument a couple of years ago in a confirmation class I was teaching to some high school students. Not surprisingly, it went the same direction as my high school conversations and ended with a similar argument. The students abandoned the issue of belief for a debate about how good we actually have to be to get into heaven. I listened to the conversation for a long time, as the young people debated with one another. Finally, I shouted out, "I believe in Ashtabula" (a small town in Ohio, on Lake Erie).

"What?" the rather startled kids replied.

"I believe in Ashtabula. I've never been there. I've never seen it. But it's on my map of Ohio. So, I believe in Ashtabula."

The class stared at me in disbelief, wondering what in the world I was talking about. Then I said, "If believing in God simply means giving assent to the idea that God really does exist, then that does me about as much good as believing in Ashtabula simply because it is on a map. It's just saying yes to an idea. Believing in the theory of gravity has more power over my life than belief in God, in this case. At least believing in the theory of gravity changes my behavior—I don't step out of third-story windows without benefit of something to break my fall. The simple assertion of believing in God does little more than lead to an argument about how good we have to be to get into heaven."

But the roots of the word *believe* are much deeper and mean much more than just asserting the validity of an idea. In our Creeds (the Apostles' and the Nicene), the Latin versions begin with the word *Credo*, which we translate into English as "I believe." Actually, the root word for *Credo* is *cardia*, the word for heart. *Credo* literally means, "I believe so that I give my heart to."

Even the Old English word for believe is *beleaven*, the same word from which we derive *beloved*. Clearly, belief, in these contexts, is much more than simply assenting to an abstract idea. "To believe" is meant to be a relational verb. To apply it then to John's gospel, we might say that those who give their heart to God, those beloved of God, already know the experience of eternal life.

Considering both the Gospel of John's image of eternal life and the other gospels' descriptions of the kingdom of God, we might summarize the New Testament meaning of salvation in this way: Salvation is an encounter, a relationship with God as revealed in the person of Jesus of Nazareth. Entering into this relationship by giving our heart, ourselves over to it, transforms us so that we see the world in new ways.

The poor and those in need matter—in fact, the least may be the most important. The reality of God's presence among us is visible in the everyday events of life, such as planting a garden, helping a stranger, celebrating a wedding, or welcoming a prodigal home. And as we comprehend the presence of God in each of these things, we get a glimpse, right here and now, of what heaven is like.

The Cross of Jesus

Any look at the New Testament view of salvation would be useless if it didn't include the cross of Jesus. The cross is central. In fact, a quick reading of Mark, the shortest gospel, reveals the centrality of the cross in the New Testament.

Mark's gospel is so short that it has no birth story—it begins instead with Jesus as an adult and moves rapidly to Jerusalem where he faces the last week of his life. The Gospel of Mark comes across as little more than a passion narrative, with a few miracle stories added on at the beginning for good measure. Mark is all about the passion of Jesus.

Saint Paul, in his letters, emphasizes the power of the cross over and over again, even saying, "I decided to know nothing among you except Jesus Christ, and him crucified" (1 Corinthians 2:2).

Crucifixion is a terrible way to die. Mel Gibson's 2004 movie *The Passion of the Christ* gave us all vivid images of just how terrible it can be. Crucifixion involves bodily mutilation from nails through hands and feet. The actual cause of death is not the bleeding from these wounds, but asphyxiation. The condemned, because of the blood loss and strain of hanging on the cross, reaches a point when he can no longer hold up his body enough to breathe, and so his lungs collapse.

In the twenty-first century, this image both attracts and repels us. On the one hand, the success of *The Passion of the Christ,* replete with graphic depictions of crucifixion, makes it obvious that many people are drawn to it. On the other hand, there may be just as many who prefer not to acknowledge that the image of the capital punishment of a condemned man is at the heart of our faith. A colleague of mine, wishing to dramatize the reality of Jesus' death as a criminal execution by the Roman authorities, placed a homemade replica of an electric chair in front of a stationary cross in his church. People were shocked, but it drove home the harsh reality of the cross, a reality many would rather not dwell upon. The crucifixion was a gruesome event, which in our day is made even more graphic and real by Gibson's film. Though many Christians went to see this movie, many others avoided the harsh depictions of violence, just like those who were shocked by the electric chair at the altar.

Christ Dying for Us

The most common theology of the cross, in our day and age, is what could be called "the substitutionary penal atonement theory." In brief, it simply means that God sent his Son to die for us, instead of killing all of us and damning us to hell for our sinfulness. This theology is preached regularly by televangelists and in most of the evangelical churches of North America. It is also the message Mel Gibson seemed to be promoting in his movie. I offer a description of the theology, with corresponding Bible verses that support it.

1. We all deserve death and eternal damnation because of our sinfulness. ("For the wages of sin is death" [Romans 6:23]; "You shall not eat of the fruit of the tree . . . or you shall die"[Genesis 3:3].)
2. God cannot forgive us our sins unless some sacrifice is made. (". . . without the shedding of blood there is no forgiveness of sins" [Hebrews 9:22].)
3. Instead of damning us to hell, out of love for us, God sends his own Son to die in our place, to be the sacrifice for our sins. ("[H]e entered once for all into the Holy Place, not with the blood of goats and calves, but with his own blood" [Hebrews 9:12], and the near sacrifice of Isaac, seen as a prefiguring of the sacrifice of Jesus on the cross as the Son of God [Genesis 22:1–19].) Christ is the only adequate sacrifice because he has no sin, and God, being perfect, cannot accept anything but perfection ("he made him to be sin who knew no sin" [2 Corinthians 5:21]).
4. Our response to this love is to believe in Jesus, to acknowledge that he died in our place, and to give our lives over to him

to go to heaven. ("Whoever believes [in me] has eternal life" [John 6:47].)

Some object to this theology because of its emphasis on the need for death and some even more so because it makes God out to be a cruel parent. God kills his own Son, just so we can be spared. It sounds grue-some and horrible. There is good news and bad news for those who do not like this theology. First, the bad news: It's the dominant theology of the cross in our day. As a result, even those who do not like this image are stuck with it. From movies to preaching, it is everywhere. Now, the good news: It is not the only theology of the cross or even the oldest theology. In fact, this penal atonement theory didn't become a domi-nant teaching of any church until 1915, when *The Fundamentals of the Christian Faith* was published. This collection of articles and essays gave structure and definition to the fundamentalist movement in Christianity. Bits and pieces of fundamentalism had been around for about 100 years, but this publication brought them all together in one place and, as a result, determined the direction of the fundamentalist movement in America throughout the twentieth century. One of the tenets proclaimed in the Fundamentals is that the penal atonement theory is the only orthodox (and therefore correct) way of under-standing the cross.

This penal atonement theory, though endorsed by *The Fundamen-tals of the Christian Faith* in 1915, predates this publication by cen-turies. But it doesn't go all the way back to the earliest days of the Church or even to the Bible. In fact, the first church leader to develop this view was Anselm, a twelfth-century theologian.

Anselm's primary source for developing this theory was the Bible. But his secondary source was the feudal society of his day. Here's why: In feudal law, the lord of the manor is the ultimate authority, and all the inhabitants of his land are his vassals. If a vassal were to in any way offend the lord of the manor by breaking the law or failing to show proper respect, the punishment was always death. Feudal society functioned that way. It was harsh and cruel, especially for the lowest of the low.

Anselm created a theology appropriate to his culture. If we are under God's control—if we are his creatures, his vassals—then to break God's laws or to dishonor God resembles offending our feudal lord. This is a sin. And since the wages of sin are death, then any sin, like any dishonoring of the lord of the manor, is punishable by death. To save us from death, God replaces our punishment with the death of his Son. The need and demand for death is satisfied. Unlike our earthly lords, the God of all creation is perfect, and so would demand a perfect sacrifice. Jesus is the perfect replacement because he has no sin and can therefore substitute sufficiently for all the sins of humanity.

Anselm simply looked around at the world he knew, read his Bible, and described the cross in a theology that all who lived in feudal society would understand. The theology made sense in such a cruel and harsh time. Then, capital punishment was meted out for even some of the most minor crimes. And if capital punishment didn't kill you, there was always rampant disease, brawling and fighting among competing vassals, war, and a host of other problems. Death was a much more constant companion to people of the twelfth century than it is to people today, so no one questioned a cruel and harsh consequence to sin as meted out by a loving God. It all made sense in that day and age.

Today, in the United States, we do not live in a feudal society. We do not serve overloads with complete control over our lives, who can put us to death on a whim. Disease and early death, though always a part of human existence, are nowhere near as rampant as they were one thousand years ago. Apart from the attacks of September 11, 2001, the wars in which we engage are not fought on American soil. As for capital punishment, most western democracies other than the United States have completely abandoned it. So, this penal atonement theory of salvation can seem cruel and harsh in our culture. It doesn't make sense for everyone today, and many cannot reconcile it with the idea of a loving God.

There are other problems, as well, with this view of salvation and the cross. For one, the demand that an offering be made for sin and the language we use about Jesus to describe him as that offering do not match with the scriptural tradition. For example, we call Jesus "the

Lamb of God" (John 1:29 and 36). He is the lamb who was slain for us, the sacrifice for our sins. There's a problem with this view if you read the Old Testament. The lamb was never used as an offering for sin. The temple priest sacrificed a bull for the sins of individuals and a goat for the sins of all the people on the Day of Atonement. How can Jesus be described as a "sin offering" and a lamb at the same time?

The lamb, instead, was always the offering for Passover, a remembrance not about forgiving people their sins, but about rescuing them from slavery and offering them new life. Now one could argue that Saint Paul reminds us how we tend to be slaves to our sinfulness. And one could say, as Paul does, that Jesus came to rescue us from our slavery to sin. Jesus could be the Passover lamb sacrificed for us. One could say these things, but it does not fit with the formula outlined in Anselm's theology.

The other problem with the theology is its nature as a formula. Formulas tend to oversimplify reality. The scriptural evidence, though, describes the cross in a far more complex way. Pointing out the difference between the letter to the Hebrews, which describes Jesus' death on the cross as a sin offering, and John's description of Jesus as the Lamb of God, demonstrates the problem of trying to define the sacrifice Jesus made on the cross according to a simple four-step formula. The Church has always believed God was revealed to us in the complex reality of a person, Jesus of Nazareth, and not in a formula.

The good news is that, despite the protestations of the fundamentalist movement, the penal atonement theory is not the only theology of the cross found in scripture and the Christian tradition.

Christus Victor

Christus Victor, literally Christ the victor, is the oldest theory of the cross and its relation to salvation. It dates back to an early theologian named Origen (ca. 200 C.E.) and certainly predates him as well. The theory, in its oldest form, can be elaborated as follows.

Humanity is under the sway of evil or Satan—that's why human beings are sinful. God, to save us from our sin, makes a deal with the devil, exchanging his Son for the destiny—the souls—of humanity.

Jesus then becomes the ransom for our sins ("the Son of Man came . . . to give his life as a ransom for many" [Matthew 20:28]). The problem the devil must face with this deal is that love freely offered cannot be destroyed by sin and evil. Hence, the devil is deceived, and the souls of all are ransomed by God's free gift of love, revealed in Jesus' willingness to offer love on the cross even to those who crucified him. John's gospel portrays Jesus' death in this way by having the crucified Jesus give a shout of triumph at his death: "It is finished." (John 19:30). The Greek word used here, *tetelestai*, could also be translated, "I did it." or "It is accomplished." or "I have succeeded."

Gregory of Naziansus went so far as to say that the love Jesus offered on the cross ransomed all souls from hell and will one day even redeem the devil himself. Gregory was a universalist, who believed that God was capable of saving all of humanity.

Augustine agreed. He called the cross God's mousetrap or hook for catching the devil. He declared that even the personification of evil couldn't destroy a love freely offered, and so even the devil could be redeemed in the end.

I recently witnessed, on television, an incredible understanding of this theology in the most unlikely of places, the animated series *South Park*. This show is filled with vulgar language and gratuitous references to any failings in our culture concerning politics, foreign policy, parenting, religion, and relationships. However, I am amazed at how well the writers know their theology. They make fun of it, yes, but they know it.

In an episode of *South Park,* the *Christus Victor* theology is examined and turned upside down. Satan challenges Jesus to a boxing match and Jesus accepts. The whole town of South Park bets on Satan, assuming Jesus will lose, making Jesus a long shot, paying huge returns on the odds. With just one punch from Jesus, Satan, taking a dive, falls down. And he tricks the entire town of South Park by betting not on himself but on Jesus, whose odds were so bad that Satan winds up taking everyone's money, turning deception into a windfall.

Like the wager in this TV show, at the heart of the *Christus Victor* theology is deception leading to an unexpected windfall. The deception in *Christus Victor* is that God does not let Satan in on the secret that love freely offered cannot be destroyed. The final vindication of that love is, of course, the resurrection. Since love cannot be stopped even by death, new life comes to the one who offers the free gift of love. And that new life becomes the gift to all who have been "ransomed" by God's offering of Jesus.

The trouble with this view of the cross is that it involves the image of Satan. And in our day and age, Christians differ on the meaning of Satan. Some describe him as an actual being, the personification of evil, as the ancient theologians do. Others view Satan as a mythic figure. *Satan* or *the devil* are terms describing certain realities in human existence, including the fact that human failure—leading to terrible consequences, from the mildest of insults to atrocities such as the Holocaust—has always been a part of who we are. Human failure never seems to go away, but lives on from generation to generation, like an eternal being. Also, the evil that we commit can be greater than the sum of our sinfulness. The Holocaust may have been the brainchild of Adolf Hitler, but it mushroomed out of control and was, ultimately, far worse than the sum of all the crimes committed by those who perpetrated it. In other words, evil seems to have a life of its own that is bigger than all of us.

Whether one believes that Satan is an actual being or a mythic one, the presence of evil in human existence is indisputable. The *Christus Victor* theology may, at first glance, seem to depend on a belief in the personification of Satan as an actual being. But there is a modern interpretation that fits even with the mythic view of evil.

The message in this theology is that God transcends our evil by not responding in kind. Instead of punishing us for our sinfulness, God over and over again offers love. This love takes form in the one we call his Son, Jesus the Christ. Jesus offers love even to those who crucify him. Such a love cannot be overcome by evil, and so it is a triumph to be offered even in the face of death.

Jesus' parable of the Good Samaritan (Luke 10:29–36) is an example of love being offered in the face of potential rejection. If we know about the realities of life in Jesus' day, then we would know that the

Jews and Samaritans hated each other. What makes the Good Samaritan story so effective is the willingness of the Samaritan to offer love and care in a situation where it most likely would have been rejected. The result is healing and goodness for the one who would have rejected the love being offered. This interpretation of the Good Samaritan parable, then, echoes the *Christus Victor* theology of the cross. Love is offered, even in the face of rejection. And the ones who benefit even include those who rejected that love.

A modern example of this kind of love, offered in the face of rejection in ways that positively transformed the ones rejecting that love, can be found in the American civil rights movement of the 1960s. Protestors offered love and respect even to those who beat them and pummeled them with water cannons. The result: the world was transformed for the better by that love, even improving the lives of those who rejected it, as the changing realities of the South led to vast economic improvement.

In theological language we can say that God's offer of love, revealed in Jesus on the cross, changed our relationship with God forever. A love freely offered cannot be destroyed. And when it is freely offered, it even changes for the better those who would reject it. The Christ is victorious.

THE INCARNATION OF LOVE

The incarnational love of God theory of salvation is rooted in Matthew and Mark, who describe Jesus uttering an incredible gasp of despair just before his death: "My God, my God, why have you forsaken me?" (Psalm 22:1).

What a contrast this is to John's gospel telling us that Jesus' final words were a shout of triumph. But if we read Mark's and Matthew's descriptions of Jesus' death in conjunction with some of Saint Paul's and John's thought, we find a very redeeming message in this cry of despair.

Paul, in his letter to the church at Philippi, declared that Jesus, though he was in the form of God, humbled himself to be found in human form and to die on the cross (Philippians 2:6–8). Later, John's gospel would describe Jesus as the Word of God made flesh among us—the Incarnation (John 1:14). If we say that in Jesus God's love and God's presence revealed itself to humanity, then we can look again at Jesus' cry of abandonment and say that even here, God's presence and love were revealed. In the most godforsaken place of life—betrayed and abandoned by one's closest friends, physically and emotionally abused, and finally killed—even here at the cross God was present.

The power of this reality moves Paul to an incredible speech in the eighth chapter of Romans that hearkens back to Psalm 139. "Nothing can separate us from the love of God," Paul proclaims. And then he lists powers, calamities, and problems of life, the universe and the cosmic order, even death. Not one of these things will ever keep us from the love of God revealed in Jesus Christ. How does Paul know this? Because he has found the presence of God even at the cross. Even at a place we call godforsaken, God is there. And because God is with us, even during the greatest pains of our lives, we can trust that God will sustain us and pull us through. After all, look what happened to Jesus after the crucifixion. The resurrection reminds us that there is no such place that is truly godforsaken.

SALVATION AND THE CROSS

The cross cannot be reduced to a formula. Jesus' death, as with the death of any public figure, is a complex reality with far-reaching implications that may never be fully understood. People still debate the meaning and impact of President John F. Kennedy's death and ask whether or not we have been told the truth about it. The death of Jesus was, over the course of humanity's existence, a far more important event. It has been interpreted in many ways across time. The reality of this event is attested to by numerous historical sources, but it transcends mere history. Jesus' death reveals the mystery of God's love. And no single theory of the meaning of Jesus death could ever capture the fullness and breadth of the love of God we claim was revealed at that time.

In our day and age, the primary theology of the cross and its connection with salvation comes from the fundamentalists' insistence that the substitutionary penal atonement theory is the only orthodox view. This theology may be helpful for many people, but it also offends many others.

A simple look at history and scripture shows a much richer tradition. Some commentators describe the cross as God's free gift of love, a love so profound that evil could never destroy it—the victory of the Christ. Still others describe the cross as representing God's willingness to join us even in the most supposedly godforsaken places of human existence. The beauty of these last two views is that they do not depend on the promise of an afterlife to make sense. Yes, we can still hope for resurrection and entry into the life to come, but these two views also make sense in this life. The victory of the Christ shows how a love freely offered can change the world, as it did not only with Jesus, but in the nonviolent movements such as the civil rights struggle in the United States, or the nonviolent resistance of Gandhi in India. And the incarnational love of God reminds us of God's presence here and now to help bring us through the toughest times of our lives.

CHAPTER 4

FROM EARTHLY TO HEAVENLY HOPE

A close look at scripture reveals that biblical understanding of salvation can't be reduced to a formula for simply "getting our ticket punched on the train to the afterlife." The early Church understood that salvation was more than just getting into heaven. But it wasn't long before an otherworldly focus began to take over.

THE BLOOD OF THE MARTYRS

The early Church spread through the Roman Empire by appealing to the poor, the outcasts, and the downtrodden. As Paul said, writing to one of his earliest churches in Corinth:

> Consider your own call, brothers and sisters: not many of you were wise by human standards, not many were powerful, not many were of noble birth. But God chose what is foolish in the world to shame the wise; God chose what is weak in the world to shame the strong; God chose what is low and despised in the world, things that are not, to reduce to nothing things that are. (1 Corinthians 1:26–28)

With the message that God loved all humanity, and that the savior was willing to sacrifice his life even for those who were the lowest in society, the Church grew. The message held enormous appeal for those of lowest degree. Suddenly, they felt important. Suddenly, they found themselves part of a community. Their lives, in this world, were transformed. They called each other brother and sister. The early Church even shared possessions in common to insure that no one went hungry. Becoming a Christian was a step up on the social ladder for many of the new converts. So, for the early Church, this gospel message was not just about getting into heaven, but about being valued, fully alive, and redeemed in the here and now, in the context of a loving, caring community.

Unfortunately, that didn't last for long. Rome began to persecute the Church early in the second century of the Common Era. At first, the persecution was isolated and focused on small areas in what is now Turkey. The main reasons for the earliest persecutions were treason and atheism—yes, atheism. That charge may sound strange, but a failure to believe in the gods of the Roman Empire was treated as a failure to believe in divinity at all. The charge of treason, however, carried the greater weight.

This charge comes from a complicated series of events in the Roman Empire over the course of the first century. At that time, citizens of Rome were expected to show their allegiance to the emperor by burning incense before his statue as they might before one of the Roman gods. This act of deference seems like little more than what we do today when we show commitment to our nation by pledging our allegiance to the flag. Incense burned to the emperor showed one's devotion to the Empire.

An exemption for this practice was given to the Jews. They claimed to believe in one god and could not therefore violate their faith by treating the emperor as a deity. The Romans knew their history well enough to know that forcing the Jews to violate their faith in any way could lead to disastrous consequences, such as constant rebellion in Palestine. After all, the Greeks learned that lesson around 165 B.C.E. when they tried to force the Jews to worship Zeus, only to find themselves caught up in a guerilla war that led them to withdraw completely from Jerusalem and the surrounding areas. We have a record of this war in the Apocrypha (1 and 2 Maccabees). The rededication of the temple after the defeat of the Greeks is remembered and celebrated annually with the festival of Hanukkah. The scrappy, defiant Jews simply would not be tamed by the world around them, which asked for their allegiance to Greco-Roman deities and symbols. And so the Romans offered them a little more freedom of religion than other nations received. They were not required to burn incense to the emperor.

Since Christianity started out as an offshoot of Judaism, it received this same exemption as well, until two events occurred that changed all that. First, the fire of Rome in the year 64 C.E. began a process of identifying Christians as separate from Jews. Nero blamed the Christians for the fire, singling them out from their Jewish brothers and sisters. Next, Rome finally got fed up with the separateness of the Jews and the constant guerilla warfare from the Zealots. Rome invaded Palestine and besieged the Jewish people in the years 66 through 70, destroying Jerusalem and scattering the Jewish people to northern and southern Palestine and throughout the Roman Empire. Being associated with Judaism became a liability for the Christians, so they began to identify themselves as different and separate from the Jews.

Now that Christians considered their religion separate from Judaism, they were no longer accorded the exemption for burning incense to the emperor, an exemption the Jews kept even after the Palestine War. Nevertheless, with roots in Judaism, Christians proclaimed a simple, monotheistic creed: "Jesus is Lord." By implication, this meant, "Caesar is not Lord." And so they refused to pledge allegiance to the empire or its lord, the Caesar. Hence, local Roman officials leveled treason charges against them.

Countless legends describe Christians willingly going to their deaths on these charges of treason rather than acknowledge any lord other than Jesus. Some of the motivation for this came from the *Christus Victor* theology of the cross. If Jesus could love those who crucified him, and if the resurrection showed that such a free offering of love could never be destroyed, then by implication his followers could do the same. And they did.

But these early persecutions were sporadic, isolated to various places in Asia Minor where the local authorities felt threatened by the growth of this new religion. For most of the first two centuries of the Common Era, Christianity was generally tolerated or ignored by Rome, at least until around the year 200. At that time, the Roman Empire, under

Emperor Septimius Severus, launched an empire-wide persecution of
Christianity. It is from the persecutions during this era that we hear the
stories of Christians being thrown to the lions. The story of Perpetua
and her companions represents one of the most dramatic. The following account is from *Lesser Feasts and Fasts*, an Episcopal Church docu-
ment that remembers the heroes of the faith:

> Vibia Perpetua was a young widow, mother of an infant and
> owner of several slaves including Felicitas and Revocatus. With
> two other young Carthaginians, Secundulus and Saturninus, they
> were catechumens preparing for baptism.
>
> Early in the third century, Emperor Septimius Severus decreed
> that all persons should sacrifice to the divinity of the emperor.
> There was no way that a Christian, confessing faith in the one Lord
> Jesus Christ, could do this. Perpetua and her companions were
> arrested and held in prison under miserable conditions. In a doc-
> ument attributed to Perpetua, we learn of visions she had in
> prison. One was of a ladder to heaven, which she climbed to reach
> a large garden; another was of her brother who had died when
> young of a dreadful disease, but was now well and drinking the
> water of life; the last was of herself as a warrior battling the Devil
> and defeating him to win entrance to the gate of life. "And I awoke,
> understanding that I should fight, not with beasts, but with the
> Devil. . . . So much about me up to the day before the games; let
> him who will write of what happened then."
>
> At the public hearing before the Proconsul, she refused even the
> entreaties of her aged father, saying, "I am a Christian."
>
> On March 7, Perpetua and her companions, encouraging one
> another to bear bravely whatever pain they might suffer, were sent
> to the arena to be mangled by a leopard, a boar, a bear, and a sav-
> age cow. Perpetua and Felicitas, tossed by the cow, were bruised
> and disheveled, but Perpetua, "lost in spirit and ecstasy," hardly
> knew that anything had happened. To her companions she cried,
> "Stand fast in the faith and love one another. And do not let what
> we suffer be a stumbling block to you."

Eventually, all were put to death by a stroke of a sword through the throat. The soldier who struck Perpetua was inept. His first blow merely pierced her throat between the bones. She shrieked with pain, then aided the man to guide the sword properly. The report of her death concludes, "Perhaps so great a woman, feared by the unclean spirit, could not have been killed unless she so willed it."[7]

Clearly, the early Church theology of *Christus Victor* was at work in the story of Perpetua. But we also see, in her visions, the beginnings of an emphasis on the next life. It was as if martyrdom was becoming a sure guarantee of entrance into heaven. In fact, one theology of the early Church held that the unbaptized, who were martyred for their faith, could consider their own blood to have the same validity and efficaciousness as the waters of baptism. So steadfast were many in their faith, even at the prospect of death, that Perpetua is not alone in the history of the Church as a martyr willing to suffer death rather than disavow her lord.

Such steadfast faith even in the face of certain death impressed many in the Roman Empire. Severus's plan to eliminate Christianity ultimately failed—because of his persecutions, membership in the Church actually increased. Many were attracted to a cause others were so willing to die for. As the old saying goes, the water that nourishes the growth of the Church is the blood of the martyrs.

Even so, some of the martyrs may have been willing to face death because the appeal of the next life was greater than that of their current existence. As noted earlier, the early Church did bring in poor people, slaves, and outcasts. They became "somebodies" in the eyes of God and found a place to belong. But becoming Christian did not always improve their social standing outside of the Christian community. As far as Rome was concerned, they were still "nobodies"; nobodies who could even be persecuted and killed. The next life may have been viewed as a desirable alternative to those conditions. Though most of our legends of martyrdom from this era speak of bravery, that may not have been the motivation of all the martyrs.

As the Church grew, later Christians would not be so brave. Around the year 250, another empire-wide persecution broke out. But this persecution took place after a time of toleration. In toleration, the Church grew beyond its humble beginnings among the lowly and outcasts. Many men and women of higher standing began to join the ranks of Christianity. When the persecutions began, Roman leaders once again threw Christians to the lions. Again, martyrs stood bravely in the face of death. But history also offers many stories of Christians recanting their faith to save their necks. These more settled Christians who took on the faith during a time of toleration may not have been so impoverished, and so they may have had more to lose. In fact, we know that even some bishops and priests backed down. We know this because of a controversy it caused in the early Church.

When the persecutions ended, many of the bishops and priests who recanted their faith wanted to return. Some in the Church wanted them thrown out. Others went so far as to say that because of the priests' and bishops' cowardice they were not worthy of the office, and in fact their unworthiness caused all the sacraments they performed before the persecution to be invalid. People baptized by the apostate clergy were re-baptized. Those ordained by the apostate bishops were re-ordained. The Church settled the dispute by saying God's mysteries and sacraments are bigger than those who administer them. Therefore, the validity of the rites of the Church never depends on the moral character of those who administer them. This is still the theology of the Church, and it represents a much more lenient stance within Christianity than prevailed prior to the persecutions of 250.

After 250, Rome fell into another prolonged period of toleration. The more lenient theology of the Church, which even welcomed back those who had renounced their faith, made Christianity more attractive, and it continued to grow. More and more, the appeal of the Church could be found in its message of the hope of heaven. By the fourth century, only one emperor felt threatened enough by this growing religion to even try and persecute it. Diocletian, in the years 304 and 305, attempted one last empire-wide attack on Christianity. He wanted to restore the Roman traditions and even the Roman gods, but he failed miserably.

The Roman gods were seen as little more than a bankrupt civil religion used to support and legitimate the state. Meanwhile, Christianity had grown so large that any attempt to destroy it would have meant destroying vast segments of the Roman populace. By the time of the Emperor Constantine a few years later, the religion was everywhere. In the year 313, Constantine legalized the practice of Christianity, and in the year 325 made it the state religion of the Roman Empire.

Once Christianity became the state religion, it began to adopt official creeds, such as the Nicene Creed (ca. 325), as standard statements of belief for all of Christendom. Priests and bishops began to serve as public figures in the community. Churches were built everywhere. And Constantine's mother, Helena, went to Jerusalem and identified various holy sites from the New Testament and then financed the building of churches there. The Empire was Christian, and a spirit of hope and optimism began to fill the Church.

THE CITY OF GOD AND THE CITY OF MAN

Despite the increasing focus on the next life that developed because of the martyrs and the general growth of Christianity throughout the third and fourth centuries, enough Christians still understood Jesus' preaching about the kingdom of God to expect something wonderful from the universalizing of Christianity in the Empire. Because of their newfound recognition and the optimism it inspired, many Christians expected that God's kingdom would now come on earth. After all, the largest empire in the known world had embraced Christianity; why shouldn't the thousand-year reign of Christ commence immediately?

As history will remind us, that didn't happen. In fact, Christianity itself broke into warring factions over the meaning of the Trinity. One group developed the formula for the Trinity, which remains standard theology to this day: This view claims that the Son of God is coequal and coeternal with the Father (the orthodox view). Another group, led by a priest named Aries, believed in the subordination of the Son of God and his creation by God at some point in history (the Arian view). The Arians and the Orthodox Christians battled mercilessly for generations, sometimes even killing one another.

In addition to this fighting within Christianity, cynicism developed over the realization that even in a Roman Empire that had turned Christian, political squabbling and corruption continued. The Christian Empire was not that different from the pre-Christian empire. Wars against the external barbarian tribes continued. Petty graft among political officials persisted, as did strict Roman law, and even the bloody games in the coliseum. Many simply adopted a cultural view of Christianity not unlike the earlier cultural assimilation to the Roman gods. For many it seemed that Rome had simply swapped one set of religions for another, and life went on as usual.

In fact, this cultural assimilation of Christianity led to the beginnings of the monastic movement. The man called the first Christian monk, Antony, retreated into the desert to get away from the watered-down, cultural acceptance of Christianity that seemed to be the norm. Some of his later followers would be called the Desert Fathers: solitary monastics seeking a deeper relationship with God than they believed was possible in the everyday world. They were soon followed by the first monastic community, that of Saint Benedict, who believed it would only be through some distance from everyday life that anyone could explore the depth of faith. Though Benedict proclaimed a life of "work and prayer," he still called for that life to be led in a community of celibates living apart from the rest of the world.

Then, in the early fifth century, the city of Rome began to suffer attacks from barbarian tribes—not only was Rome failing to behave in a Christian manner, it also appeared to be under attack and declining. Many wondered where God was in all this. Rome had not become the kingdom, even when it became Christian. Some Christians began to believe they could not live a true life of faith unless they removed themselves from the everyday life of Rome. And now the eternal city was under attack. What did it all mean?

Saint Augustine responded with his book *The City of God*. In it, he points out that the City of God and the City of Man can never be the same thing. Rome could never be totally associated with the kingdom of God, no matter how Christian it was, because the kingdom of heaven and the kingdom of earth will never fully merge in this life. Yes, we pray, "thy kingdom come, thy will be done, on earth as it is in heaven," but we cannot expect it to arrive this side of heaven. Yet even if we cannot expect complete consummation of God's kingdom in this life, we are obligated by our faith and values to work for such a kingdom.

Augustine's reasons for declaring the impossibility of attaining the kingdom were twofold. First, if we, by our efforts alone, could create God's kingdom, then we would take credit for it ourselves rather than giving the glory to God. Then, it wouldn't be God's kingdom but ours. Second, human sinfulness, or what Augustine called "original sin," is an ever-present reality that always trips us up, infecting every human action with the potential for error.

Now, in its purest sense, the idea of original sin is simply the acknowledgement of a human reality. Just as experienced when Rome embraced Christianity, it seems obvious that all human efforts at goodness fall short of the ideal. Something always holds us back. Augustine called this "original sin," but as I like to say, "There is nothing original about sin. It has always been around and we keep repeating the same mistakes." We are not perfect. We cannot attain perfection, either as individuals or as empires or as countries. That is the truth of original sin.

Augustine complicated the concept, however, by associating it with procreation. He declared that the mere act of procreation and birth assure that original sin will be passed from generation to generation.

Augustine also defined a cure for Original Sin: baptism. Once we are baptized, God, in essence, washes away the stain of original sin, and we are made acceptable in God's sight. Though we still live in an imperfect world, by virtue of our baptism we are perfectly suited for God and assured of an entrance into the resurrection life.

In creating this theology, Augustine was, on the one hand, describing his experience. We live in an imperfect world that doesn't appear to improve even when populated by Christian people. On the other hand, he was trying to make sense of that reality in the face of what the Bible and Christian tradition claimed was the experience of salvation. We are saved, but our salvation does not make us completely perfect, at least not in this life.

Augustine was simply describing reality as he saw it. He lived in a Christian empire that failed to become God's kingdom, God's empire on earth. Then, Augustine developed a theological concept, original sin, to explain why even a nation of people experiencing the salvation of God could not be perfect, could not create God's kingdom on earth. In the end, Augustine created a theology that would remain the dominant understanding of the faith throughout the Middle Ages. However, this theology quickly degenerated into a formula for salvation with an almost exclusive emphasis on the next life. From the time of Augustine onward, everything in medieval Christianity centered on the hope of heaven as only the resurrection, only the next life, based on Augustine's formulas concerning original sin and baptism.

The formula that developed went something like this:

1. Original sin made it impossible for us to be perfect and therefore impossible to be acceptable to God.
2. Baptism washed away the stain of original sin, making us acceptable in God's eyes, and therefore worthy of heaven, even if imperfect and still living in this imperfect world.
3. Even though we are baptized we still sin, so we need to regularly seek God's forgiveness through confession.

Eventually, the Church began to elaborate on this formula by classifying some sins as mortal, saying that one's immortal soul was in danger if one died with an unconfessed, unforgiven mortal sin. In addition, the idea that unbaptized babies could be denied heaven seemed cruel to many, so a place called limbo was created in the Church's theology regarding hell. Limbo was neither heaven nor hell, but a place where the innocent unbaptized, especially infants, would go upon death.

Thus began an overwhelming emphasis in the life of the Church on matters of heaven and hell. If we could not attain the kingdom on earth, then all that seemed left for us was to hope for it in heaven. We received that hope at our baptism, but could be denied it by our behavior: our mortal sins. This view affected the theology of every aspect of the medieval Church. It affected confession. We must confess our sins and receive forgiveness or risk the loss of heaven. It affected the medieval Church's theology of the Eucharist. One could not receive communion without being made worthy enough to receive this sacrament through confession and absolution. It affected the theology of marriage. If one conceived children out of wedlock, then they could not be baptized in the church itself but only on the steps of the church. An examination of church records from the oldest churches in Europe will show that most of the serfs and vassals were not married, because so many of their children were baptized on the church steps rather than in the building itself. A child born of such sin could not be brought into the church, but neither could it be denied the sacrament that would wash away the stain of original sin and even the stain of the sin of its conception. The Augustinian view of original sin and the need for its cleansing away through baptism, confession, and absolution even affected the Church's view of burial. Anyone who committed suicide could not be buried by the Church because, after all, suicide is a mortal sin committed without the hope of confession and absolution. Therefore, the victim's fate was already determined. Why should the Church bother with a service?

I do not believe Augustine expected this kind of development in his concept of original sin. After all, Augustine was a universalist who believed that even the devil could be saved. Remember that it was Augustine's theology that described Jesus' death on the cross as God's victory of love—a love offered even in the face of rejection, even to the devil himself. Augustine simply tried to create a theology based on his experience of the perpetual imperfection of humanity. His theology soon became a formula used by the Church to determine who would make it to heaven and who would not.

This view survived the decline and fall of the Roman Empire. It survived the changes in European culture that replaced Rome with many small kingdoms, which eventually transformed into the countries of modern Europe.

When Dante wrote his *Divine Comedy* (ca. 1300), which metaphorically describes the afterlife in great detail, he didn't invent a new theology, but rather used the popular theology of his day about limbo, hell, purgatory, and heaven, with its roots in the Augustinian theology of the Middle Ages. His poem was intended as a work of art that describes the spiritual journey: how we move from being lost and in limbo, through confession of our past unfaithfulness (hell), to a purging of sin (purgatory), and finally to a greater appreciation for our salvation in the nearer presence of God (heaven). Dante used afterlife images to describe the journey of spiritual growth. Nevertheless, his incredibly elaborate descriptions of heaven and hell give us a glimpse of how much the medieval Church and popular theology emphasized the next life to the exclusion of all else.

By the early sixteenth century, this theology of the afterlife became so elaborate that the Roman Catholic Church even used it as a fund raiser. The Church sold indulgences. These were guarantees by the Pope that deceased persons would be relieved of the torments of purgatory if one of their living relatives contributed to the Church's coffers. In other words, the Church turned its formula for salvation into a formula for self-perpetuation and profit.

It was this formulaic understanding of salvation that Martin Luther rebelled against, developing the Protestant theology of salvation by God's grace alone. Though Luther rebelled against the Church, he remained an Augustinian through and through. Like Augustine, he believed that we would never fully reach the kingdom in this life. Like Augustine, he admonished his followers to work for that kingdom, even if we do not attain it completely. But even Luther accepted the reality of the persistence of human sin. The best example of his acceptance of sin's ability to limit our attaining the kingdom in this life revealed itself in the peasant revolt of 1524. The peasants, buoyed by Martin Luther's proclamation of salvation through grace alone and by his insistence that we work for the kingdom even if we do not attain it, decided to revolt against their overlords to seek relief from their poverty and misery. In the end, and for the sake of order, Luther wound up supporting the overlords in putting down the revolt, compromising with the reality of human sin in this life by supporting the imperfect kingdom of the overlords to the neglect of the poverty of the peasants.

As a result of the Protestant Reformation, beginning with Martin Luther, Christianity began breaking into even smaller factions. However, all of these groups still seemed obsessed with the meaning of salvation as it applied to the next life. It took the crossing of an ocean to restore emphasis on the meaning of salvation in this life.

CHAPTER 5

HEAVEN ON EARTH?

For hundreds of years, the formulaic baptismal theology of Augustine and the Middle Ages dominated the Church and pushed its emphasis on salvation into the next life. Even the infighting of Christianity over the meaning of salvation, which led to the Protestant Reformation, was largely a battle over the destiny of human souls in the life to come. While Luther talked about the hope of heaven, Calvin went so far as to say that those destined for heaven were "predetermined" by God from eternity. Christianity was all about the next life. Nevertheless, an emerging strain of Christianity hoped that the kingdom of God might be revealed in the here and now, as it hoped for, and worked for, glimpses of heaven on earth. The story of that strain of the faith begins with the earliest history of the country that now proclaims a separation of church and state: the United States.

A City Upon a Hill

John Winthrop, an early governor of the Massachusetts Bay Colony and one of the early Puritan settlers in New England, gave a sermon on board the ship *Arbella,* on his way to the "New World." He outlined what the Puritans hoped to accomplish in coming to America and how their work would be regarded by others: "For we must consider that we shall be a city upon a hill. The eyes of all people are upon us."[8]

Winthrop, of course, was referring to Jesus' Sermon on the Mount (Matthew 5:14), where Jesus admonishes his followers to be an example to the world around them. The Puritans hoped to create a new society, based on pure religious doctrine and discipline, which would be an example of how Christians should live with one another. In essence, they sought to create a utopia, the kingdom of God on earth. In coming to a new, "unspoiled" country, with nothing more than the basic necessities for life and a strong desire to do the right thing, they believed nothing could stop them.

The examples of the failure of this movement are legion, from history books to novels like *The Scarlet Letter* by Nathanial Hawthorne. We know that by the late seventeenth century, the Puritan movement sank into a dark time of paranoia that led to the Salem witch trials.

How could a movement with such promise fail? The theological answer comes from Augustine's *City of God*: that the potential for human error infects every human action. In the case of the Puritans, their desire for right behavior, as a prelude to right community, led them to persecute and punish any individual who did not live up to expected standards. They turned Christianity from a religion of hope and promise, a promise of the kingdom of God, into a religion that demanded conformity or the consequence of harsh and cruel punishment.

When I teach classes on the history of the Church, many people ask, "Whatever happened to the Puritans anyway?" The answer surprises them. The Puritans are the ancestors of the United Church of Christ and the Congregationalists, the most liberal Christian denomination in the United States. It is the only mainline Protestant denomination to officially allow for openly gay clergy and formally recognize the blessing of same-sex unions. People ask, "How could such a morally strict group become so liberal?"

The answer can be found in the Puritans' origins as a group seeking the kingdom of God on earth. They still remain true to that goal. In the early days, the Puritans thought they could bring about the kingdom by observing very strict morals and beliefs. Today, they try and realize the kingdom by seeking to build a better world, a more open and progressive world, that cares for those who are lowly and outcast. The goal remains the same—to serve as an example of how to proclaim and live into God's kingdom, to be a "city on a hill." Only the methods have changed.

Utopia in the Wilderness

While serving a church in Hudson, Ohio, I worked on a committee planning celebrations for Hudson's two hundredth anniversary and came across an interesting fact about the town's founding. Reading the area's history, I was surprised to find that David Hudson came to the wilderness to start the town that bore his name as part of a religious quest. He described himself as a selfish, ambitious man who eventually saw the light of the gospel and decided to mend his ways and start a new life. He was encouraged by his pastor to seek solace in the wilderness, to go out to the unexplored territory as a quest for the renewal of his soul. Just as the Israelites were transformed by their dependence on God through wanderings in the wilderness, so David Hudson hoped that his soul would be strengthened and renewed by similar wanderings in an unfamiliar land.

Reading this history reminded me of a group I learned about on a trip to New Harmony, Indiana, some twenty years earlier. I'd received an invitation to attend a meeting sponsored by the National Episcopal Church on churches in small communities. Upon arriving, I found a number of surprises. First of all, this little town with a population of less than a thousand sported an opera house dating back to the early nineteenth century. What a surprise, I thought, an opera house in such a small town in the middle of nowhere. A road sign pointed to the "Open Air Church." I had a few minutes before I needed to check in at the conference, so I drove by the church. There I found a four-walled, brick church with no roof. It was open to the sky, as if open to the gaze of God. All over, various sculptures adorned a snow-filled sanctuary. It was beautiful, and here in the middle of nowhere. Finally, when I got to the conference center, I noticed a grove of trees that looked like a small meditation garden or shrine. I walked over and found the grave of the great theologian Paul Tillich.

I was beside myself. I had never heard of New Harmony, Indiana. Yet this little town held an opera house, a beautiful artistic piece of art and architecture called the Open Air Church, and even the grave of a famous theologian.

The conference center told it all, providing a small exhibit and library on the history of New Harmony. Apparently, it had been founded by a group of separatist German Lutherans, under the leadership of a man named George Rapp. The community came to Indiana in 1814 with the express purpose of creating a Christian utopia in the wilderness—the kingdom of God on earth. Through work, prayer, and shared property, these Harmonists, as they were called, hoped to live into God's kingdom in this life. They were quite successful, by societal standards, creating a functioning community and generating a substantial amount of wealth, which was shared by the whole community. But because the goods and agricultural products the Harmonists sold had a better market back east, they sold the community in 1825, moved back to Pennsylvania, and eventually were absorbed into the society around them.

The group that bought New Harmony, under the leadership of a Scot named Robert Owen, continued much of the utopian idealism but developed the town into more of an intellectual ideal rather than just an agrarian paradise. They provided schooling opportunities for all ages and built the opera house. Eventually, this group was absorbed into the Progressive movement, popular throughout the later nineteenth and early twentieth centuries in rural Middle America.

However, New Harmony remained as a reminder of the utopian movements that sought to bring about the kingdom of God on earth in the midst of the American "wilderness." Tributes can be found to their idealism in the Open Air Church, the grave of Paul Tillich, and a modern state park that describes the town's history.

The Harmonists and Robert Owen were not alone. Many utopian societies formed throughout the nineteenth century, the most famous being the Shakers of Kentucky. They separated themselves from the world and tried to create a perfect society. What differentiated the Shakers from other utopian communities is that they expected the imminent second coming of Jesus. They figured they didn't have long to wait before the kingdom they were creating on earth was merged with the heavenly kingdom at the end of time. In a sense they were trying to create a utopia, a kingdom of God on earth, so that when the second coming did happen, they would be prepared, living as if they had already arrived there.

Because of this expectation of the second coming, the Shakers also practiced complete celibacy. This was to abide by Jesus' description of heaven as a place where the eternal are not given to one another in marriage (Mark 12:25). In other words, they were preparing on earth for what they expected heaven to be, and this included the abolition of marriage, and as the Shakers interpreted it, the abolition of sex as well.

Unfortunately for the Shakers, the second coming did not take place. And because of their strict rule of celibacy, they slowly died out without heirs, at least as far as we know.

I was first exposed to the Shakers as a teenager. On a family vacation we stopped at the Kentucky state park called Shaker Village where we had a chance to experience the structure of the community and the contributions the Shakers made to life in rural Middle America. They were known for wonderful cooking, and the beauty of Shaker architecture influenced much of the building in the Midwest as it grew beyond a wilderness. To demonstrate a little humor about the group's rule of celibacy, my parents had me take a picture of them in the community dorm. Apparently, the dorm was set up for both men and women. Despite their celibacy, the two sexes ate together in the refectory on the first floor of the building, but they slept separately on the second floor. Two separate sets of stairs led up to the sleeping quarters, one side for men and one side for women. My parents asked me to take a picture of them at the bottom of the stairs. The twist is that in the picture my mother is standing at the bottom of the stairs to the men's dormitory and my father, the women's. The picture remains in the family photo album to this day as an inside joke for us all to enjoy.

All the utopian movements died out. The Shakers died because of celibacy. The Harmonists and others were absorbed into the culture. But they did have an influence on the world around them. In some ways, the Harmonists paved the way for the Progressive movement that longed for greater community influence on politics and supported public education for all people. The Shakers, through architecture and food, helped give a cultural basis for a settled Midwest, and less radical forms of Christianity adopted pieces and parts of their utopian philosophies.

After all, the nineteenth century was a time of incredible optimism about humanity. A social doctrine of progress was developing, which assumed that human life would progress into better and better forms as technology and knowledge grew. Churches, in some ways spurred on by the utopian movements and influenced by the cultural expectation of human progress, began to make efforts to improve the world around them by making it more like the kingdom of God. Churches began to build schools, even in the poorest sections of major cities. They built hospitals, even for those who could not pay for health care. If humanity were to progress, then the Church had to facilitate that progress by making sure even the lowest of the low had access to the improving lot of all humanity.

My own denomination, the Episcopal Church, offers numerous examples in its history of this straining for the kingdom in the midst of the nineteenth century's cultural expectation of human progress. William Augustus Muhlenberg founded the Church of the Holy Communion in New York City as a means of reaching out to the poor and dispossessed in the city. He abolished pew rental, provided a local school, founded St. Luke's Hospital, and even organized trips to the country for city children. Muhlenberg's story was repeated in large urban areas all over the United States, not only in the Episcopal Church but in many other denominations as well. The Girl's Friendly Society, a group of church women who made themselves available to young, single women moving to the cities to find work, developed in my church as well. The church women would offer support, welcome, and a degree of security and would generally watch out for these young women alone in the growing urban environment. In other words, the older women of the church befriended younger women who were alone and vulnerable.

Other denominations made similar efforts, as the Presbyterians, Baptists, Methodists, Lutherans, Catholics, and others built schools, hospitals, settlement houses, and facilities to care for those in need. All of this was seen as a part of the Church's mission. The Catholic Worker

Movement, the Salvation Army, and numerous other societies sought to bring relief to the poor in the rapidly growing urban centers of the nation. Thus, the Church worked for glimpses of the kingdom even here on earth.

A THEOLOGY FOR THE KINGDOM OF GOD

By the turn of the twentieth century, the ideal of human progress so filled the imagination of North America and Western Europe that the actual efforts of people working for the good of humanity translated itself into a full-fledged theological theory of heaven on earth. Walter Rauschenbusch, a Baptist theologian from Colgate Rochester Divinity School in Rochester, New York, published *A Theology for the Social Gospel* in 1917. Though he was the one who elaborated a concise and clear theology for why the Church should work for the kingdom of God on earth, Rauschenbusch was not alone in this theology. He simply became the spokesperson for a variety of views popular in his day.

Rauschenbusch pointed out, as I did in the previous chapter, that much of Christianity's history had forgotten about any efforts to work for the kingdom: "The doctrine of the Kingdom of God shriveled to an undeveloped and pathetic remnant in Christian thought."[9] The Church, according to Rauschenbusch, had abandoned the kingdom that Jesus proclaimed and exchanged it for Church buildings, institutional survival, and an obsession with the next life.

To regain its soul and be true to the preaching of its founder, Jesus of Nazareth, Rauschenbusch called on the Church to work at making the world a better place. And in his theology he proclaimed that simply seeing that churches were building schools, or hospitals, or caring for the poor in the street was not enough.

> The Kingdom of God is not confined within the limits of the Church and its activities. It embraces the whole of human life. It is the Christian transfiguration of the social order. The Church is one social institution alongside the family, the industrial organization of society, and the state. The Kingdom of God is in all these, and realizes itself through them all.[10]

Thanks to the theology of Rauschenbusch and others, members of the Church began to politically lobby for the eradication of child labor laws, for laws ensuring public education, and public health. They wanted to use the modern world, including government and industry, to bring the kingdom on earth.

In many ways, future efforts like the New Deal, under Franklin Roosevelt, and the Great Society, under Lyndon Johnson, owe a debt of gratitude to this theology. Such efforts used the public structure of society to promote the values of Jesus' message of the kingdom of God. Though the United States government's doctrine of separation of church and state would never allow for an explicit identification of these social policies with any religious views, the similarity between the New Deal, the Great Society, and the theology of Walter Rauschenbusch cannot be denied.

There was one major problem with Rauschenbusch's theology. It was published just as the United States entered World War I. That bloody war was the beginning of the end for the doctrine of human progress in western culture. And if the First World War was not enough to kill it, the Second World War, with the Holocaust and the first use of atomic weapons, completely obliterated the idea. How could anyone believe in a doctrine of human progress after trench warfare sent millions of young men to horrible deaths—all to gain a few feet of land in a war that resolved nothing? How could anyone believe in a doctrine of human progress with six million Jews and three million others systematically killed in response to a madman's dreams of a master race? How could anyone believe in a doctrine of human progress when the progress of humanity led us to build weapons of such power that we stood on the brink of annihilation?

After World War II, the United States held on to an optimistic view of humanity and hope for the future. After all, other than Pearl Harbor, the world wars had been fought on the soil of other nations. We felt a sense of satisfaction and triumph in winning World War II. The postwar economy raised the standard of living for the vast majority of Americans, and hope blossomed everywhere. But even that hope seemed to die in the face of Vietnam, the cultural revolution of the

1960s, and the Watergate scandal. And so the theology supporting the creation of God's kingdom on earth faded from the public mind.

One vestige of Rauschenbusch's theology did come back to influence the world, even in the midst of the death of the doctrine of human progress. It came from a student at Rauschenbusch's seminary, about a generation after the theologian's death. A young black preacher from the South named Martin Luther King Jr. received a degree from Colgate-Rochester Divinity School. Fully schooled in the theology of the Social Gospel, King sought to create a society where a "man was judged not by the color of his skin but by the content of his character." And so the civil rights movement owes a debt of gratitude to Rauschenbusch as well.

Despite the New Deal, the Great Society, and the civil rights movement, the theology of the Social Gospel could not help but fall victim to the reality Augustine reminded us of so long ago. Any attempts to create the kingdom of God on earth will never fully succeed because of the reality of human sin. We cannot be perfect this side of heaven.

Yet let us not forget the second part of Augustine's theology. Though we may not create the kingdom on earth, we are not absolved from trying. We can use the values of Jesus' proclamation of the kingdom to reach for a better world. Though we cannot create utopia, we can succeed from time to time at making the world a little better, a little more like the kingdom. When I teach classes in the churches I've served, I often say that working for the kingdom in this life is actually preparing us for the next as well, just as the Shakers believed. After all, the Shakers wanted to prepare for the imminent convergence of the afterlife with this one in the second coming. We, on the other hand, can prepare for the afterlife through glimpses of God's kingdom in the here and now. If we can strive for and envision God's kingdom in this world, then perhaps we will recognize it after the resurrection as well.

KINGDOM MOVEMENTS REVISITED

In some ways, the Puritan ideal of creating a "city on a hill" has been revived in our day and age in two very different and distinct ways.

The first way in which the image of the city on a hill returned to the public imagination was thoroughly secular. Ronald Reagan, during his

presidency, described America with those same words from John
Winthrop's sermon, quoted at the beginning of this chapter. For Reagan, America was, in fact, a shining city on a hill. But rather than claim-
ing this as a religious cause, our fortieth president gave it the nuance of
secularism. The shining city on a hill was an example not of God's
kingdom but of democracy, economic prosperity, the war on communism, and freedom.

When President Reagan died, Supreme Court Justice Sandra Day
O'Connor read Winthrop's sermon as a part of Reagan's memorial
service at Washington National Cathedral. By doing so, she set into historical context the phrase that so characterized the Reagan presidency.
The image of the shining city on a hill has become so secularized that
many of the people I talked to after those services were surprised to
learn that Reagan had taken the words from a sermon. Still more were
surprised when I told them the words were actually a quotation from
Jesus' Sermon on the Mount.

The second way in which the city on a hill theology has been revised
comes from a thoroughly religious perspective. Remember, the Puritans thought they could bring about heaven on earth, or a close
approximation of it, by emphasizing right behavior. If the Christian
community could just live by a proper moral code, then the right and
just community would naturally follow.

Today, we still have groups within popular Christianity that empha-
size this desire for right, moral, Christian behavior. The Christian
Coalition represents the most successful political group supporting
this agenda—they have generated substantial influence within the
Republican party. During the entry into the Iraq War of 2003, the
Christian Coalition even supported the idea that God had called
George W. Bush, an Evangelical Christian himself, to the White House,
as a way of promoting God's will on earth.

In addition to supporting politicians they deem to hold the most
Christian values, the Coalition also promotes various kinds of legisla-
tion to make our nation more Christian in its morality. They are
opposed to abortion and gay rights and in favor of prayer in schools.
The Christian Coalition's attempts to legislate moral behavior, unlike

those of the Puritans, are not about creating the kingdom of God on earth, but about converting the world to Christianity in order to get as many people as possible into heaven. Chapter 6 will explore this agenda more thoroughly.

Whether by seeking to make the world a better place through social welfare and the transformation of society or by seeking to legislate moral, Christian behavior, the Church has sought God's kingdom even in the here and now. If society were just better, we would be closer to that kingdom, we believed. Or, we proclaimed that if only human beings were more moral, more aligned with Christian values in their personal behaviors, then the kingdom would be at hand.

Such efforts have led us to prohibit child labor, to improve working and living conditions, to make provisions for the needy, to establish a system of health care for the elderly, to equalize the application of our laws among the races, and a host of other social reforms. Such efforts have also led to moral crusades on issues such as temperance and abortion.

Augustine admonished us that we would never fully attain the kingdom in the here and now, but that hasn't stopped Christians from trying. Though most of modern Christian theology tends to emphasize the hope of heaven as only pertaining to the next life, the social and moral reforms made by people of faith throughout history attest to our striving for God's kingdom on earth.

CHAPTER 6

∞○∞

THE NEW VIEW OF SALVATION

I couldn't believe what I was hearing. A parishioner in a congregation I served over ten years ago declared, "My guess is that well over half of the people who come to this church aren't really even Christian."

When I asked her how she could say such a thing, she explained that she believed people needed to have a conversion experience and invite Jesus into their hearts before they could be considered Christian. What about the act of communion, I asked, whereby parishioners take the bread and wine, as representative of the presence of Jesus, into them? Doesn't that count as a kind of altar call, or the invitation of Jesus into one's heart?

She accused me of being flippant and declared that most people wouldn't view communion like that anyway. "And what's more," she said, "they can't be Christians because they don't believe the truth about the Bible."

I responded by reminding her that after every reading of scripture in our church, the reader says, "The Word of the Lord."

"Yeah," she said, "but that doesn't mean they believe it. To believe it's the Word of the Lord, they have to believe it's all factual, and that what was spoken by God was what was written by the authors."

The conversation was beginning to have an edge to it. I got the impression this parishioner was even starting to question my legitimacy as a Christian, let alone as an ordained minister. I replied, "What you've just described is not the doctrine of the Episcopal Church but of fundamentalism. In the Episcopal Church we believe that God inspired the *human authors* of the Bible, but not that it was all dictated to them."

"Then I am shocked to learn that the Episcopal Church, the church I have attended all my life, isn't even Christian," she declared and left my office.

I was stunned. I'd never heard such theology in the Episcopal Church. I remember my parents and others describing us as "the thinking man's church." I'd always understood the Episcopal Church as a place that allowed for questions and for broad interpretation of the Bible and of doctrine. I'd always understood the Episcopal Church as a church that didn't require a rigid adherence to a literal interpretation of scripture. I'd always understood the Episcopal Church as willing to apply the methods of historical analysis and criticism to scripture without being threatened by such inquiry.

Unfortunately, that conversation I had some ten years ago has been repeated numerous times between me and other lifelong Episcopalians. One person even went so far as to accuse me of heresy, simply for teaching something I had learned in seminary—that the Gospels may not have been written by the people whose names are ascribed to them. After all, we have no signed copies of the Gospels. As Raymond Brown, a Roman Catholic theologian at Union Seminary, teaches in his book *The Churches the Apostles Left Behind*,[11] the Gospels may have been assembled from various oral stories and histories in the communities where the apostles lived and died. For example, Matthew's gospel may have been assembled in the church community where Matthew was. After his death, the people began to pull together the things he had told them that they found most important. In a sense, it is not Matthew's gospel but the community of Matthew's gospel, Brown argued.

"Heresy," said this lifelong Episcopalian. "The Apostles wrote those books."

To which I replied, "If you are accusing me of heresy, then you're accusing every Episcopal seminary and Raymond Brown, a great theologian, of heresy."

He said, "Then so be it, because they're all wrong."

Why have some lifelong Episcopalians abandoned our church's heritage of study, reflection, and open interpretation, and instead have adopted stances more akin to fundamentalism? And why do they assume that this is what the Episcopal Church should believe or always has believed? I think it comes from the way in which the public face of Christianity has changed over the last fifty years.

Fifty years ago, the household names of Christianity were C. S. Lewis, Norman Vincent Peale, and Bishop Fulton Sheen. Lewis was an Anglican; Peale, a Presbyterian; and Sheen, a Roman Catholic. Representing mainline, traditional churches, they constituted the public face of Christianity. Lewis wrote about the transformative nature of following Christ, how it made our lives better (*Surprised by Joy*) and how we could be ethical people (*Mere Christianity*). Peale wrote about trusting God and the hope for a better life (*The Power of Positive Thinking*). And Sheen, through his radio and TV programs, encouraged Catholics to use prayer, such as the rosary, and the Church's liturgies, to sustain them in their daily lives.

That was the description of Christianity I remember from my childhood. None of these authors made drastic calls for doctrinal adherence. In *Mere Christianity*, Lewis simply made a philosophical argument for why we should believe Jesus is who he said he was. Though Lewis himself did experience a rather profound conversion, he never made his own story a requirement for others to follow. These authors all taught Christianity as if it were a given for all those who claimed it, and then they offered advice on how to make their Christian lives better. Though they counted on a hope for the life to come, they were very much attuned to living in the here and now.

Needless to say, Lewis, Peale, and Sheen are not the public faces of Christianity today—they have been replaced by Billy Graham, Pat Robertson, and Jerry Falwell. All three of these men are fundamentalists, ascribing to the doctrine that the words in the Bible were spoken by God into the ears of those who wrote them, and that they should be taken literally and factually. All three are conservative evangelicals who believe that one must be able to point to a day and time of conversion, when one made a mature decision to accept Jesus as one's personal savior.

Because of these men there has been a subtle shift in emphasis over
the last fifty years. It began with Billy Graham's rise to fame and the
success of his preaching missions around the world. Then, it was
amplified by television and the power of people such as Robertson and
Falwell to raise vast sums of money and place their worship services
and talk shows on cable channels all over the nation. Then, with the
success of the Christian Coalition in influencing the Republican party
and the growth of the megachurch movement, fundamentalist, conservative Evangelical Christianity has become the norm. This is now
the public definition of our faith.

Those who are unchurched, or those who have drifted from church
since their childhoods, assume this is the meaning of Christianity. I am
always amazed when visitors come to the Episcopal churches I have
served and are surprised by what they find. They are surprised to see a
liturgy with set prayers, because that doesn't look like the worship services they see on TV; often they ask if we are Catholic. They are surprised by interpretations of scripture that are not literal, because that
is not what they hear on TV. They ask if we really believe in or follow
the Bible, since we do not have sermons calling for rigid adherence to
the Bible as a scientific and historical book of facts.

But the strange thing that has happened because of this shift in the
public view of the faith is that many mainline church members have
adopted the fundamentalist view uncritically and simply assume that
is what their church has always believed. At first, I was surprised by the
encounter I described at the beginning of this chapter. But now, as I've
come to understand how the public definition of Christianity has
changed over the years, it's no wonder there are more fundamentalist,
conservative evangelical members in the pews of the churches I serve.
They have taken our culture's current public definition of Christianity
and applied it to the Christian church they attend, and they assume
that is the way it has always been.

I was finally convinced of this radical shift in the public definition of
Christianity when I visited a major bookstore chain to buy a Bible. My
copy of the *Oxford Annotated, New Revised Standard Version* was wear-
ing thin. It had been fully used up in my study and preparation for

preaching and was falling apart at the seams. When I went to buy a new copy, the book was not available. There were plenty of Bibles, but not a single New Revised Standard Version. Instead, there were dozens of different editions of the New International Version (a favorite translation of the fundamentalist and conservative evangelical movements) and of the King James. There was not even a version of the Revised Standard (which the New Revised replaced in 1991). The NRSV is the Bible translation most often used in the mainline Protestant denominations. It is the one referred to in most of the mainline seminaries for training their clergy. If bookstore chains respond to the buying power of the majority, then clearly the majority is not in step with mainline Protestantism.

This change in the public definition of Christianity is the main reason our view of salvation has become so oriented on the next life. Christianity now focuses almost exclusively on what we need to do to get into heaven, because that's what the fundamentalists and conservative evangelicals preach. Believe the right things, do the right things, in order to be guaranteed a place in the next life. Yes, groups like the Christian Coalition support the Puritans' ideal of right community coming from right behavior. They believe that changing the laws of the United States around issues like sexuality, abortion, and prayer in schools will make us a better nation. But the emphasis is not on creating the kingdom of God on earth or the Puritan vision of the city on the hill. Instead, the emphasis seems to be on creating a "Christian nation" that might then be an example for converting the world to Christianity, not for the sake of this life, but to get everyone to heaven in the next.

One reason those who support the current public definition of Christianity are so concerned about converting the world and getting everyone into heaven has to do with the newfound obsession with the second coming of Jesus. Like the early Church and, later, the Shakers, the fundamentalist and conservative evangelical churches are convinced that we are living in the very final days of this physical world, and that Jesus' second coming is right around the corner. Witness the incredible popularity of books and movies based on Tim LaHaye and

Jerry B. Jenkins's *Left Behind* series. The series offers a fictional account of what might happen after the "rapture."

The rapture is a concept recently developed in Christianity, based on two verses of scripture from Paul's first letter to the church in Thessalonica. It says, "For the Lord himself, with a cry of command, with the archangel's call and with the sound of God's trumpet, will descend from heaven, and the dead in Christ will rise first. Then we who are alive, who are left, will be caught up in the clouds together with them to meet the Lord in the air" (1Thessalonians 4:16–17).

An entire Christian culture has grown up around these verses, as believers expect a point in time when people will disappear from this world to be immediately snatched up into heaven. Then, a time of tribulation and conflict will follow. There is debate in the Evangelical church as to whether anyone can be saved or guaranteed heaven after this "rapture." Some say yes and others no. But at some point after the rapture, Jesus will come decisively to end this physical world and begin the heavenly one.

Those of us in the mainline churches believe, just as modern scientists do, that this physical world will come to an end. But as Christians we believe the spiritual world will endure beyond it. We do not, however, believe that now is necessarily the time when that will happen. We believe what Jesus said in the Gospel of Matthew: "But about that day and hour no one knows, neither the angels of heaven, nor the Son." The mainline churches also do not adhere to this fairly recent development of the doctrine of the rapture.

Because the rapture and expectations of the second coming have become dominant in the public understanding of Christianity, there is now little concern for this world. Why should we be concerned with the physical world when it will end soon? This seems to be a popular attitude. In fact, in the 1980s, the Secretary of the Interior, James Watt, an Evangelical Christian, was purported to have said that we really didn't need to care about the environment because of Jesus' imminent second coming. It is no wonder all the emphasis seems to be on the next life. Believe the right things, do the right things, in order to get into heaven, because soon that may be all there is.

Therefore, the puritanical desire for right behavior in our country has very little to do with creating a city on a hill, as in creating the kingdom of God on earth. Rather, it is all about converting the world to Christianity before it is too late, saving as many as possible to assure them a place in heaven.

Old Problems with the New View

There are problems with the current public definition of Christianity. First, it is restrictive. It requires a strict doctrinal adherence to such things as a literal interpretation of scripture and the need for a defined conversion experience. Because we in the traditional, mainline denominations do not require this same kind of strict doctrinal adherence, at the very least our validity as Christians is questioned, and at the worst we are publicly condemned as unchristian. I can remember far too many sermons I have seen on television, or heard on the radio, from fundamentalist pastors railing against the mainline denominations for compromising the faith. The Episcopal Church is often a target because it allows for questioning and interpretation. As I have said more than once in sermons and teaching opportunities, because of the Episcopal Church's openness and willingness to take on such tough issues as sexual orientation, we are viewed by many as "the poster child for the moral decline of the mainline denominations." Granted, a church being open to discussion on moral issues, rather than taking a clear moral stance, is a legitimate target for criticism as a fencesitter, or for being morally "mushy." But to reject us altogether hardly promotes any sense of mutual Christian unity or understanding.

As part of conservative Christianity's challenge to the Episcopal Church, I once heard a radio sermon complaining about a crucifix in the Cathedral of St. John the Divine in New York City that depicts a woman on the cross. The statue is called a "Christa." The preacher complained about the mainline denominations simply rewriting the Bible and Church history to fit their own liberal agenda. I called the pastor who gave the sermon to challenge his public complaint. I asked him to consider the piece not as a rewriting of the Bible but as an artistic rendering of a theological truth.

"What truth?" he asked in a hostile manner.

"Do you believe that in the incarnation of Jesus, God joined humanity, even in humanity's suffering?"

"Of course," he replied.

"So," I went on, "if God shares in our suffering, does he also share in the suffering of women, especially the abused, raped, and forgotten?"

"Yes, but Jesus was a man."

"Of course, I don't think anybody would deny that. This was just an artistic rendering to remind us that God shares in our suffering, even the suffering of women."

"But Jesus was a man," he insisted again.

Needless to say, he was not convinced of my interpretation.

A few years after that encounter, I tried to build a relationship with the pastor of a local megachurch. The church he served was strongly fundamentalist and very conservative in its understanding of evangelism. The two of us were trying to find a way to work together to support the community we served as it wallowed through a bitter labor dispute between the school board and teachers. We had lunch together and found many things to agree on to help the community. We would pray together, work together to promote dialogue between teachers and administrators, and hold public gatherings to encourage reconciliation and peace. We did all of those things. This megachurch pastor even came to services at the Episcopal Church I served. But in our initial lunch he made sure to remind me of his views regarding the mainline denominations. He said he was glad we were working together on this issue, but that he had been taught in seminary "that you [the mainline churches] are the enemy."

So, the current public definition of Christianity is restrictive. It does not recognize all of those who claim the name of Christian as "truly" Christian. As a result, the current public definition of Christianity, by its very nature, promotes conflict. Conflict exists between mainline churches and those who view us as "the enemy." And there is conflict within mainline churches as more and more people in the pews simply adopt the current public definition of the faith and begin to apply its restrictive attitudes to their fellow Episcopalians, Methodists, Presbyterians, Catholics, Lutherans, and others.

There is another problem with the public definition of Christianity, but first I must offer a disclaimer. I accept fundamentalist, conservative Evangelical Christians as my brothers and sisters in Christ, even if they do not accept me in the same manner. I believe they have an important role to play in Christianity. They appeal to those who desire certainty in their faith. They appeal to those who could not experience the transformative power of following Jesus without some decisive conversion experience that radically changes their lives. I am more than willing to welcome fundamentalist and conservative evangelicals into the churches I serve. But I do tell them, "You and your theology are welcome, but not an attitude that treats your fellow parishioners as not 'truly' Christians."

Since I recognize those who support the current public definition of Christianity as my brothers and sisters in Christ, my criticism of them and their theology is offered not as a rejection but as a warning. I believe that the current public understanding of Christianity is just as destructive to the soul as the works righteousness Martin Luther rebelled against in the sixteenth century, and that unless we can change this understanding, we will cause more harm than good with our faith. To explain what I mean by this, let me first describe the works righteousness Martin Luther rebelled against.

WORKS RIGHTEOUSNESS THEN AND NOW

Martin Luther was a tortured soul who feared going to hell. He was a monk who subscribed to the medieval model of Christian salvation— that salvation was guaranteed by baptism, unless one died with an unconfessed, unforgiven mortal sin on his soul. Young Martin went to confession constantly to be sure he did not die with a mortal sin on his soul.

He was afraid of purgatory, too. Purgatory, in Roman Catholic theology, is the place between this life and the life to come, where our sins are "purged" from us in order to make us fit for heaven. After all, nobody dies perfect, and if we are to be accepted into the eternal presence of a perfect God, then something has got to change. It was reasoned that there must be some place where our sinfulness is "purged" from us for eternity. Dante, in the *Divine Comedy*, described purgatory as a place almost like hell in terms of punishment. But such punishment was viewed as necessary to transform us into the heavenly people we would become in the next life. It was thought that since we would spend eternity in heaven, then we might spend thousands of years in purgatory preparing. Martin was afraid that his sins would lead to a long period of "purging" in purgatory.

Because of his fears of hell and purgatory, Martin constantly doubted the legitimacy of his salvation. He worried that he wouldn't be worthy of eternal life or worthy enough to pass quickly through purgatory.

But there was a way out. In Martin Luther's day, the Pope was granting people "time off" from the thousands of years of purging. This "time off" could be purchased by means of something called an indulgence. The indulgence was signed by the Pope and could be purchased on behalf of a deceased relative, presumably someone who was already in purgatory, or it could be purchased on one's own behalf. The money it cost to purchase the indulgence was sent to Rome to help build Saint Peter's Basilica.

While reading Paul's letters, Martin Luther had an epiphany. As he read passages such as "[W]hile we still were sinners Christ died for us" (Romans 5:8), "For by grace you have been saved through faith" (Ephesians 2:8), and Paul's description of grace as the "free gift" of God (Romans 5:15), he couldn't help but think that God was generous, caring, and loving, and desired humanity's salvation above all else. Suddenly, Luther realized his salvation didn't depend upon how many times he went to confession, or how much he avoided sin, or how many times he went to church, or how many indulgences he bought. His salvation depended on God alone. His only response to this free gift was gratitude, trust or faith in God, and a desire to live like a person loved by God. Though he could formulate a response to this free gift of love—gratitude, faith, living a new kind of life——he also realized these things did not make his salvation happen. He already had salvation. His response was simply a way of appreciating God's gift more and more.

Once Luther realized the graciousness of God, he suddenly was struck by the miserly love of humanity, even by those who claimed to serve God. In his ninety-five theses, his objections to the teaching of the Catholic Church in his day, Luther especially attacked indulgences. He asked: If the Pope indeed has the power to free tortured souls from the ravishes of purgatory, then why doesn't he just do it out of love, rather than for money?[12]

Luther's criticisms of the Church made sense to many, and the Protestant Reformation was born. His ideas made so much sense in terms of what scripture tells us about the love of God that even the Roman Catholic Church exonerated him and accepted most of his teachings about grace by the end of the twentieth century.

Unfortunately, for much of modern Protestant theology and especially the theology attested to in our common public understanding of the faith, we have abandoned Martin Luther and adopted a whole new form of works righteousness. No longer is purgatory the great threat, but hell still is. And the current public definition of Christianity proclaims that all who are not "saved" are going to hell. Then it describes all kinds of prior "works" one must do in order to be assured of salvation and avoid eternity in hell.

Today, Christianity seems to be all about avoiding hell and getting into heaven. Here, in no particular order, are some of the formulas I have heard, either in sermons or from my fellow Christian pastors who ascribe to these views, describing the necessary preconditions for salvation:

- You're not saved unless you can point to a day and time when you gave your life over to Jesus and invited him into your heart. Or, as a friend of mine puts it, "You're not saved until you say the Jesus prayer." By that he means some kind of personal, extemporaneous prayer about giving your life over to Jesus. Reciting the Baptismal Covenant or the Creed in a mainline church does not count, because these are written prayers that are not truly from the heart.

- You're not saved unless you believe that the Bible is the literal word of God, that he spoke it into the ears of the writers, and that it reports completely factual events. The most extreme version of this I heard in a radio sermon from the most successful megachurch in my hometown. The preacher said that believing in a literal six-day creation was necessary for salvation, and that all those who even thought of evolution as a viable alternative were damned to hell. I encountered a strange twist to this precondition for salvation from another pastor, who once questioned the legitimacy of my salvation. He gave me an interesting variation on the prerequisite of Biblical literacy. He asked, "When you were saved, was it done with a King James Bible? It doesn't count unless it's done with a King James Bible." Apparently, I was not saved unless I happened to be convinced of the truth about Jesus from one and only one translation of scripture.

- You're not saved unless you believe in the substitutionary penal atonement theory of the cross, as outlined in chapter 3. People who question this theory of atonement as gruesome or hard to reconcile with a loving God are immediately considered "doomed to hell" by those who push this precondition. And even when other historically valid options to this theory are offered, they are rejected as not fitting with the necessary requirements for salvation.

The problem with all of these statements is that they put preconditions on God's salvation. They put human expectations on what we have to do or believe, or think, or agree to, before God can give us the "free gift" of love. In other words, it gives us work that we have to do in order to make our salvation happen. It is no different than what Martin Luther rejected when he rebelled against the popular definition of Christianity in his day that demanded confession and indulgences.

As I work with confirmation classes and try to teach them about the concept of God's love and grace as free, and about all the preconditions we put on it as works righteousness, I ask the following question: "If we put preconditions on our behavior or beliefs before God can love us or save us, then who determines our salvation?"

"We do," they say.

And then I respond, "So salvation is a product of our behavior or our beliefs. God doesn't have anything to do with it. We're totally in charge. We don't even need God, except as the dispenser of the salvation we've earned."

That answer usually doesn't sit well with them. But I push the matter and point out that God is always in charge of our salvation. It is always God's free gift. We cannot determine it or make it happen. If we could, then we could have saved ourselves. And one of the doctrines of Christianity is that we cannot save ourselves. We need God.

Martin Luther taught us that every time we put preconditions on our behavior or beliefs that determine our salvation, then we have adopted a theology of works righteousness. We have turned salvation into something we can somehow manipulate and control. But since we are sinful, imperfect human beings, this kind of theology always leads to doubts about whether we have done everything right, believed everything right, or done the right "works." Deep down we know we are not perfect. So deep down we wonder if we can ever do the things necessary to be saved. This theology led to doubts for Martin Luther, and it leads to doubts for people today.

I know this because I encounter souls as tortured as Martin Luther's among the young people in the congregations I have served. Many young people in mainline churches have friends who attend the more fundamentalist and conservative evangelical churches. These friends challenge the legitimacy of the salvation of kids from churches other than their own. And they issue statements that begin, "You're not saved unless. . . ." Sometimes young people say these things to one another out of a sense of concern, but at other times their words contain a challenge or a sense of arrogance that implies, "I'm better than you because I am a Christian" (and by that they mean the right kind of Christian).

Some of the young people who live in this kind of environment (and this kind of environment has been created in the high schools of all the communities I have served as a pastor) are filled with doubts. In the innocence and uncertainty of youth, they wonder if they are doing the right things with their faith. Some, like Martin Luther, become desperately afraid of going to hell, and they want to do all the right things to make sure they avoid it. Their doubt causes great anguish and great fear of God rather than a longing for or love of God. And I believe such overly fearful worrying about our salvation is destructive to the soul. Unfortunately, it is the current popular definition of Christianity that promotes such destructive worrying.

Martin Luther taught us that such worrying is useless. And to paraphrase Martin's challenge about indulgences, I ask those requiring prerequisites to salvation, "If you can grant salvation because of the preconditions you set on it, then why don't you just offer it to everyone out of a sense of love rather than as a challenge and threat?"

BELIEF AS SALVATION

How did we reach this point of saying that belief has to be a work or precondition for earning salvation? It seems that Christian faith has been reduced to demanding that unless we believe in things that may seem outlandish to some—like a literal six-day creation—then we have somehow abandoned the faith. Salvation has come to equal believing strongly in things we might normally have doubts about. And so the more strongly we believe things that science or reason may cast doubts upon, the stronger is our faith?

It reminds me of an old *Peanuts* cartoon where Linus is explaining the Great Pumpkin to Peppermint Patty. As soon as he finishes telling Patty his theology—that the Great Pumpkin rises out of a sincere pumpkin patch in order to bring toys to all the good little children on Halloween—Patty says, "That's the dumbest thing I've ever heard." And then she shouts, "But I believe it!" This even surprises Linus, and he asks with shock, "You do?" Is this what we have reduced salvation to? Believing no matter what?

I think part of our problem is that we have confused the words *belief*, *religion*, and *faith*. Look up each of these words separately in a thesaurus and you will always find the other two. But we have forgotten that they all have distinct and different meanings.

Belief means assent to a fact or idea as something real. For example, when it comes to facts, we can believe in the theory of gravity. It has been proven factual by countless scientific studies. We can believe that gravity is real.

We can also believe in ideas. Ideas cannot necessarily be proven by scientific study, but we can still say that they are "true," not in a factual way but perhaps as good ways of looking at and living in the world. For instance, we can believe that "Honesty is the best policy," or "Virtue is its own reward."

So belief is about facts or ideas, things that we trust to be true.

Religion is not the same as belief but rather it is what we do—how we act and behave—as a result of our beliefs. For example, if we believe in the theory of gravity, then our "religion" in relation to gravity is to take stairs and elevators from one floor to another in order to avoid stepping into thin air. If we believe that honesty is the best policy, then our "religion" is to tell the truth.

In relation to God, what we believe will determine our religion. It will determine what we do because of our beliefs. If we believe God is our creator, then we will offer praise and deference as creatures of that God. If we believe that we must one day give an account for our behavior before God's judgment, then we will try to align our behavior and morals in ways we hope will be pleasing to God. Hence, belief determines religion. But belief is not a substitute for religion, and neither should it be considered a prerequisite for salvation. Rather, belief is a way of describing how we approach salvation. We believe there is a God and that God loves us. If we believe such things, then we will look for ways in which God's love is revealed to us, through the gift of life, through the gift of the love we share with family and friends, and through a hope for salvation (being made right with God). In essence, beliefs help us become aware of our salvation. Beliefs help us make sense of our experience of God. And the experience of God's love is meant as a gift that comes even before we believe anything, not as a consequence of our right belief.

Declaring that we have to believe certain things as a precondition for salvation is like saying we have to understand obstetrics before we are born, while we are still in our mother's womb. Making sense of the process of birth comes after the experience, not before. The same is true of salvation and belief. We describe our beliefs and doctrines as a way of making sense of our experience of the love of God. We don't decide to believe certain doctrines before we can even get God to love us. In essence, to paraphrase Jesus, beliefs and doctrines were made for humanity, to help us understand God's love for us, not humanity for beliefs and doctrines.

As for the concept of *faith*, I find it to be a much more complex idea than that of either belief or religion. In the ancient biblical languages of Greek and Hebrew, *faith*, *faithful*, and *faithfulness* were all the same word. We may mistake the word *faith* for *belief*, but once we begin to use words such as *faithful* and *faithfulness*, then *belief* is not a good synonym. Rather, words like *commitment*, *relationship*, *marriage*, *fidelity*, and *allegiance* come to mind. Faith is about a commitment to something or someone. If we have faith in God, it does not just mean we believe in God or that we believe all the right things about God. Instead, it means we are in a relationship with and committed to God. If we remain faithful to God, then it means we keep that relationship alive even during times of doubt and struggle. In some ways, we can compare faithfulness to God to faithfulness in a marriage. The best married couples, those we admire and would like to emulate, are not people without struggles and doubts. Rather, they are people who have remained committed to each other even through those times.

As I like to say about belief, religion, and faith: Belief can bring us to God, religion connects to God, but it is faith that keeps alive a relationship with God even when belief and religion fail. But contemporary Christianity holds up the idea of belief as the most important of these three words. Many Christian commentators even declare certain beliefs as prerequisites for salvation.

We have reached this state of affairs at least in part because of the scientific revolution of the last three hundred years. Since the time of Sir Isaac Newton, we have been living in a world obsessed with finding the facts about how the universe works, how tiny particles work, how genes and microbes function, and so much more. Because we have delved into the mysteries of the universe in ways that remove all the mystery and make these things facts to be manipulated, we have changed the world. We have harnessed the power of steam, fossil fuels, and the atom. We have eradicated diseases, repaired bodies, and made artificial limbs and organs. We have explored the realities of the universe from the birth of stars to their death.

Our obsession with scientific fact has created a whole new world, but it has also created a bias for truth as fact. Belief, again, is simply assent to an idea or fact as real. In many cultural circles, facts are held in higher esteem than ideas because facts cure diseases, harness power, and describe the universe. Ideas, on the other hand, may or may not be helpful. They may or may not be meaningful to people. We can believe in one set of ideas on a given day and in another set the next. Ideas can be proclaimed as "true" while at the same time contradicting one another. For example, some "truths" about life include "Waste not, want not" and "You can't take it with you." Which is true? Save for a rainy day, or use it or lose it? Ideas as truths have nuances and require interpretation. They may embrace the paradoxes of life. They are, in essence, unprovable.

In recent years, the Christian religion has been subject to this bias of declaring facts to be better truths than ideas. For example, if any biblical account, such as the story of the creation, is called a poetic metaphor that shows our dependence on God as the creator of all life, then somehow calling this account a metaphor diminishes its value as "truth." Real "truths" must also be facts, seems to be our current thinking. Fundamentalist Christianity clearly supports this view. The truth of the Bible, according to fundamentalists, is only confirmed if it also reports facts.

I find this view of scripture ironic. After all, it is fundamentalism that constantly battles science over how we teach creation and history in our schools. Fundamentalism would rather have the events of the Bible taught as historical and scientific facts. Yet it is from the scientific revolution that fundamentalists received the idea that only facts can carry the full weight of truth. Such a bias has more to do with Galileo than with God.

To capture the fullness of truth in Christianity, we must look beyond our bias toward fact. At the heart of our faith is the story of a God who loves us. And love, like the truth of an idea, can be multifaceted, open to interpretation, and filled with paradox. Now we turn to the meaning of that love.

CHAPTER 7

∽०∽

RADICAL GRACE AND THE FREE GIFT OF GOD'S LOVE

It saddens me that the current, dominant form of Protestant Christianity has abandoned its Protestant roots for a new kind of works righteousness. Today, salvation seems to require having enough belief, or the right kind of belief, before we know we're saved. We need to revive Martin Luther's understanding of grace and salvation as the free gift of a generous and loving God rather than the result of our meeting a list of prior qualifications having to do with our beliefs, attitudes, or even behaviors.

Putting preconditions on grace means that it ceases to be God's gift. Instead, grace becomes some kind of commodity we can manipulate. If it is all up to us and how we believe or act, then what do we need God for, except as the dispenser of the salvation we feel we have a right to anyway? This point of view makes salvation out to be some kind of competition, the winnings of which only go to the best in belief or behavior. That hardly seems like a faithful relationship with a generous and loving God.

To explain the generosity of God, I love to teach and preach about the parable of the laborers in the vineyard. In this parable, Jesus describes the extravagant nature of God's love and the challenges this love makes when we arrogantly place preconditions on salvation.

For the kingdom of heaven is like a landowner who went out early in the morning to hire laborers for his vineyard. After agreeing

with the laborers for the usual daily wage, he sent them into his vineyard. When he went out about nine o'clock, he saw others standing
idle in the marketplace; and he said to them, "You also go into the
vineyard, and I will pay you whatever is right." So they went. When he
went out again about noon and about three o'clock, he did the same.
And about five o'clock he went out and found others standing
around; and he said to them, "Why are you standing here idle all
day?" They said to him, "Because no one has hired us." He said to
them, "You also go into the vineyard." When evening came, the
owner of the vineyard said to his manager, "Call the laborers and
give them their pay, beginning with the last and then going to the
first." When those hired about five o'clock came, each of them
received the usual daily wage. Now when the first came, they
thought they would receive more; but each of them also received the
usual daily wage. And when they received it, they grumbled against
the landowner, saying, "These last worked only one hour, and you
have made them equal to us who have borne the burden of the day
and the scorching heat." But he replied to one of them, "Friend, I am
doing you no wrong; did you not agree with me for the usual daily
wage? Take what belongs to you and go; I choose to give to this last
the same as I give to you. Am I not allowed to do what I choose with
what belongs to me? Or are you envious because I am generous?" So
the last will be first, and the first will be last. (Matthew 20:1–16)

Everybody receives the same pay, even those who do the least. It is as if
the work doesn't matter but only the desire of the landowner to be
generous. In this parable, the landowner wants people he can give his
money to more than he wants labor. The ones who are upbraided are
those who put preconditions on how the landowner *should* dispense his
generosity. Hence, the parable reminds me of Martin Luther's insistence
that attaching prerequisites to salvation is like human beings placing
demands on God's generosity. God's generosity is also the theme of the
parable of the wedding banquet. When the invited guests don't show
up, the steward is encouraged to bring the people in from the byways
and lanes—anybody can come to the party (Matthew 22:1–11). Again,

the parable implies that the gift being given (the wedding banquet) is more important than the preconditions (an invitation).

In John's gospel we don't hear parables from Jesus but rather we see signs by which Jesus' powers are revealed. At the wedding at Cana, Jesus turns water into wine (John 2:1–12)—so much of it (about 180 gallons) that the guests can't consume it all. Again, what seems most important is the overwhelming generosity, not any preconditions for receiving that generosity. Everyone at the wedding has access to the wine. There is more than enough for everyone. Jesus' power is first revealed in John's gospel through this limitless generosity.

Martin Luther saw this incredible, generous love of God in Paul's letter to the Romans. As for me, over and over again I see Jesus, in the Gospels, displaying a generous God who seems far more interested in loving and reaching out to humanity than in applying preconditions or demanding good works. Yet our current public definition of Christianity denies this incredible, free gift of God's love and instead turns it into a formula for works righteousness little different from the medieval formula Martin Luther rebelled against. Such an attitude causes uncertainty among our young people and promotes conflict among Christians. It is a dangerous and destructive path we are on, one not worthy of the graciousness of our God.

How generous is our God with this gift of love? Let's turn to the same biblical author who so inspired Martin Luther, Saint Paul, and his letters.

Paul's View of Saving Grace

The mainline churches haven't been kind to Paul in recent years, and for two reasons. First, those who claim that we in the mainline are not truly Christian cite Paul to say one has to believe all the right things before one is saved. "We are saved by grace through faith" becomes we are saved by having enough belief or the right kind of belief—that is, if you believe in the literal interpretation of scripture, then you are saved. And the second reason we mistrust Paul is because his attitude toward women comes across as backward if not downright misogynist. After all, Paul tells the Corinthians that "women should be silent in the churches" (1 Corinthians 14:34).

But Paul gets a bad rap. These complaints can't hold up to any serious scrutiny. For example, for his time, Paul's attitude toward women was remarkably progressive—we can't fault him for failing to be a twenty-first-century feminist (another example of presentism as described in chapter 2). What is happening is that some Christians are using Paul's attitude toward women from his day and time as a prescription for how we should behave in our far more progressive era. It is not Paul but rather the way in which Paul's writings are used that is the problem. Those who deny women roles of authority in the Church often cite Paul's requirement that "women should be silent in the churches." Yet, they forget how Paul treats women as equals and says that in Christ we have transcended the obstacles to unity created by gender, social class, or ethnicity (Galatians 3:28).

We also read Paul negatively when we fail to see the generosity in his language about salvation. His concept of being saved by grace, through faith, is far more compatible with Jesus' parables and signs about the generosity of God than may first meet the eye.

Lost in Translation

To understand the generosity and love of the God that Paul proclaims in his letters, let us first look at how the Bible is translated. Some translations of Paul's letters do seem to support our current bias toward works righteousness, such as his hallmark statement that we are saved by grace through faith. But if we return to the original Greek texts, this bias is not so readily evident. The oldest texts we have of our Bible are in Greek and Hebrew, and as we have made the jump across time and language to English, sometimes important things have been lost in translation.

To appreciate this reality, we first need to understand that we read the Bible backward. In other words, as we saw in chapter 2, we read the Bible as if it were written last week, to conform to all our current preconceived notions about life, truth, reality, and faith. That's not all bad, as long as we're aware that we're doing it. For example, the Nicene Creed was written in the year 325, partly as a guide to how to read the Bible. The Creed claimed that God was revealed to us as a Trinity: three persons (Father, Son, and Holy Spirit) but one God. Nowhere is the Trinity explicitly described in the Bible, but the Creed is a lens through which we read the Bible in order to see and understand the concept of the triune God. Through the Creed we read the Bible backward across time.

The Creed is the most explicit way in which we're encouraged to read the Bible backward, basing our understanding on what we've learned since the Bible was written down. But more subtle changes in the way we read the Bible have also been introduced by the way we translate the ancient texts into contemporary languages. We have, in fact, changed the way we translate the biblical books from their ancient texts based on knowledge gained since those texts were written.

I first came across this phenomenon when I was learning Greek in seminary. I am not a Greek scholar, and much of my knowledge of Greek has faded since leaving the halls of graduate school, but three events in my Greek studies still stand out in my memory. The first was an assignment to translate the Lord's Prayer from Greek into English. It seemed like a pretty innocuous task—an exercise to test our skills at translation. But I was shocked when I realized that all the verbs in the Lord's Prayer were imperatives—demands placed on God. It was not "Give us this day our daily bread," but rather, "Give me bread, now!" Every time we utter the Lord's Prayer, we are not just humbly making a supplication before God. In my case, a lifetime of speaking these words quietly and reverently had determined the prayer's meaning. My current day bias, based on quietly kneeling and reverently saying this prayer in worship, had determined its meaning.

The Greek version isn't so meek and reverent. It's all about giving demands and orders. Jesus is giving us permission to demand sustenance—bread—from God. But Jesus is also telling us that by using his prayer we can insist that God forgive us in the same way we forgive others. That may be a demand we would hesitate to make.

The second—and most surprising—event of translation came from an assignment to translate Mark's account of the Resurrection (16:1–8) from Greek to English. Again, I thought this would be a simple exercise, but I was in for a shock. When I came to verse 6, where the young man in the tomb tells the women about Jesus' resurrection, I translated his words as "He has been raised."

Wait a minute, I said to myself. That doesn't fit with what I've always heard. We always say, "He is risen." Why do we translate it differently than what the text says?

So I went to my King James Bible. Verse 6 read, "He is risen." I went to the New International and the Revised Standard versions. They were a little closer: In each the young man says, "He has risen." At least they caught the past tense of the verb. But the verb was more than just past tense. It was also a passive verb, which requires some version of the "to be" verb in it. There was no other way to translate the Greek than to say, "He has been raised."

I went to my Greek professor, David Hawley, and asked him why the biblical translators would deliberately translate the Bible in ways other than what was actually written. His response: "The Creed."

Since we view God as a Trinity, he explained, and since one part of the Trinity is the Son, the Son must fully reveal God. A passive verb makes it sound like God the Son is being acted upon rather than doing the acting himself as a manifestation of the all-powerful God.

"And how," Professor Hawley asked rhetorically, "can an all-powerful God be acted upon?"

So, the biblical translators had simply taken into account the Creed and changed the text in order to make it fit the Creed's theology. The all-powerful God cannot be acted upon but must initiate his own actions—he couldn't have "been raised," but rather he must have risen. It may have been an error in translation, but it was an error made to uphold a theological truth of the Church.

The translators of the New Revised Standard Version of the Bible (1991) have corrected this error. They now translate verse 6 as "He has been raised." They assume that those of us reading the Bible can draw our own conclusions based on knowing the Creed and the Gospels, and they do not feel the need to manipulate the text on our behalf.

My assignments on the Lord's Prayer and the Resurrection account were my first encounters with translating the biblical text based on later understandings of the Christian faith. But the most startling revelation of how translation was affected by later attitudes in Christianity came when I was translating Paul's letter to the Galatians. Over and over in this letter, Paul tells the Galatians they are justified or saved through faith in Jesus Christ (2:16, 2:20, 3:22). That fits with our understanding of Paul in the contemporary public view of Christianity. We are expected to have the precondition of faith, or of believing the correct things, before we can be justified or saved.

The problem with this view is that it is does not agree with the text. In the Greek text, Paul tells the Galatians they are saved by (the) faith *of* Jesus Christ. And to their credit, the translators of the New Revised Standard Version of the Bible offer a footnote that shows this as a possible translation. To understand this problem of translation it takes a short Greek lesson. Let us try to make sense of this issue, which has been carefully examined by such noted biblical scholars as Lloyd Gaston and Raymond Brown[13] as well as by the entire translation committee of the New Revised Standard Version.

The words "faith in Jesus Christ," written phonetically in Greek, are *pistis* (faith) *Yesen Christen* (Jesus Christ). That is not what is found in the Greek text of Galatians 2:16, 2:20, or 3:22. Instead, it reads *pistis Yesu Christu,* which can be translated "faith (or faithfulness) *of* Jesus Christ." In other words, Paul is telling the Galatians that they are saved or justified not by their own faith but rather by the faithfulness of Jesus. First, let us look at how the translation of the text was changed, and then we will examine the implications of a more realistic—and faithful—translation of the Greek.

The first to change this text in Galatians was Jerome, who translated the Bible from the Hebrew and Greek texts into Latin in the fifth century. Jerome simply changed the word *of* to *in*. Perhaps he sought to make the text conform to Paul's letter to the Romans, which uses the phrase "faith in Jesus Christ." Romans, after all, is Paul's definitive work of theology. It may have been the last letter he wrote. And clearly in Romans Paul says that we are saved by faith *in* Jesus Christ. Paul is telling us we need to make a commitment, we need to have a relationship with Jesus, and we need to be faithful. Jerome simply made Galatians conform to Romans.

But remember that when Jerome translated the Bible into Latin, the medieval formulas for salvation were already beginning to develop, The Church was trying to create prerequisites for our salvation, and the idea that we are saved by Jesus' faith rather than our own removes the need for such prerequisites. So Jerome may have harmonized Galatians with Romans as a way of conforming to the prevailing attitudes of the Church. Later translators simply opted for Jerome's harmonization and overlooked the differences in the Greek.

Today, modern biblical scholars have returned us to the original Greek text, which proclaims a message of salvation we desperately need to hear.

The Free Gift of Grace

Why would Paul tell the Galatians they are saved by the faith *of* Jesus rather than through the faith in Jesus of each and every individual in that church? To understand this, we need to understand to whom Paul was writing.

The church in Galatia was confused. It was made up of Gentiles (non-Jews) who converted to Christianity. These Gentiles may have already been exposed to the Jewish God. They may have been what the Jewish historian Josephus called "God fearers,"[14] Gentiles who had given up on the vast, sprawling religions of the Roman Empire, which seemed to indiscriminately adopt all the gods of the nations it conquered. The Roman pantheon of deities simply expanded with the number of countries conquered. But the idea of just one god appealed to the "God fearers." Some may have wondered what it took to become Jewish or to be seen as "righteous," "justified," or "saved" by this god. Did they need to keep kosher? Did the men have to be circumcised (a painful proposition)?

Then, along comes Paul, with his message of grace and the love of God. He told these Gentiles that they were already welcomed and loved by God through the life, death, and resurrection of Jesus. They didn't need to keep kosher. The men didn't need to be circumcised. They were welcomed into the people of God by the free gift of love found in Jesus. That was Paul's gospel, and it appealed to the God fearers in Galatia.

But apparently some in the early Church hadn't gotten the message about Paul's idea of free grace. Somehow, the Galatians became convinced they needed to keep kosher and that the men needed to be circumcised. Then, and only then, the Galatians came to believe, would they be saved.

When Paul realizes what has happened, he is furious. He calls the Galatians "foolish" (Galatians 3:1) and says, "I wish those who unsettle you would castrate themselves!" (Galatians 5:12). That's pretty strong language. But after these outbursts, Paul reminds the Galatians that keeping kosher or getting circumcised will not afford them salvation. Instead, trusting in God's love for them is their true and only hope. It is not the works of the law, Paul tells the Galatians, but rather the faith of Jesus Christ that saves them.

Isn't that amazing? Paul is taking all responsibility for earning salvation away form the Galatians—it's not about them, or anything they do, he insists. It is all about Jesus and *his* faith. And how would Paul describe that faith? He would say that Jesus was faithful, even unto death on the cross (Philippians 2:8). Or, as he tells the Galatians, "It was before your eyes that Jesus Christ was publicly exhibited as crucified" (Galatians 3:1). What exactly Paul means by this phrase, we can't be sure. We know the Galatians didn't witness the crucifixion, just as Paul probably hadn't. But we can infer from reading all of his letters that the cross of Jesus was at the heart of Paul's theology. The cross would have been central to what Paul preached in Galatia while the Church was first forming. Perhaps Paul is referring to his original preaching in Galatia when he says, "It was before your eyes that Jesus Christ was publicly exhibited as crucified." Paul's preaching and writing declares that it was through the cross and Jesus' willing acceptance of it that God's love was revealed. In a sense, Paul was the first theologian to proclaim the theology of *Christus Victor*, which we looked at in chapter 3. The Christ is victorious because he offers the love of God even to those who would reject it: ". . .while we were still sinners Christ died for us" (Romans 5:8). Such a gift is our salvation because rejection can never triumph over a love freely offered. God's love, as revealed in the faithfulness of Jesus, will always win out in the end.

Paul appears to be saying to the Galatians, "Your salvation comes not from anything you do, not from any works of the law, not from observing kosher laws nor from circumcision, but from the love of Jesus Christ, offered faithfully even in the face of his death on the cross. It is a gift freely given that cannot be manipulated or controlled by human behavior. All is grace, pure grace, and the act of following some law—any kind of law—has nothing to do with it. You are saved by the faith or faithfulness *of* Jesus Christ."

It is not law but grace that saves us, Paul insists. But when we modern Christians read this language in Paul, we make a terrible mistake. We tend to think Paul is talking about the difference between the Judaism of his upbringing (law) and the Christianity he later advocated (grace). We tend to think law equates with Judaism and grace with Christianity. Those assumptions would make sense if Paul's letter to the Galatians, and all his other letters, were being written to Jews, telling them to abandon their religion of law for the grace of following Jesus. But we forget that Paul was writing to Gentile (non-Jewish) converts to Christianity. The people Paul admonishes not to be obsessed with law are not Jews at all. We forget that, and instead use all of Paul's talk about law and grace to punish our Jewish ancestors in the faith.

After all, when we read the Gospels, we encounter Jesus' challenges to the scribes and Pharisees of his day. Jesus did tend to denounce some of his fellow Jews for allowing the law to be more important even than God, the giver of the law. As Jesus said, to challenge this obsession, "The Sabbath was made for humankind, and not humankind for the Sabbath" (Mark 2:27).

But when we read Paul's diatribe against the law, we forget he is talking to non-Jews and assume he is condemning and rejecting his own heritage. As a result, my guess is that all Christians have heard sermons declaring the following: Judaism is a religion of laws, where one has to follow all the rules about keeping kosher and observing the commandments in order to earn God's love and salvation; on the other hand, Christianity and the message of Jesus represents a religion of grace where we do not have to earn our salvation, but simply trust in the love of God. I have heard many sermons along these lines and even preached a few before going to seminary. Unfortunately, this is a terrible parody of Judaism.

I remember when I first realized how totally inaccurate this description of Judaism really is. I was working for the Reverend Dr. Philip Culbertson, my seminary professor of pastoral theology. He was writing a book on the parables of Jesus called *A Word Fitly Spoken*, which examines Jesus' parables from the perspective of the writings of rabbis who were his contemporaries. It asks the question, What can we learn about Jesus' parables by examining how other rabbis from his time used this same method in their teaching?

One day, Dr. Culbertson invited a local rabbi (who was also helping with the book) to come to our pastoral theology class. I shared with this rabbi the common misunderstanding of Judaism that so many Christians believe. I wanted to know what he thought of the way Christians interpreted his faith.

He was silent for a long time after I asked the question, and then said, "Why did God choose Abraham?"

We were all stumped. Just hearing the question made the whole class realize that there was no reason given in scripture. God just called to Abraham, and he responded.

Then, the rabbi went on to say something along these lines: "You Christians like to think we Jews are trying to earn our salvation by following all the commandments, and that the only way we receive grace is by following the law. But grace is all over the Hebrew scriptures, what you call your Old Testament. It was by grace that God chose Abraham—just because of God's love for humanity and his desire for a people to call his own. It was by grace that God saved his people at the Red Sea, not because they were good or just or anything else, but simply because they were the children of Abraham. And, believe it or not, it was because of grace and love that God gave us, his chosen people, the law. After all the great things God did for us, we needed to show our gratitude. And we didn't know how to show a gratitude equal to all that God had done on our behalf. And so God gave us another gift, a means, a method of showing how grateful we are for the love and grace of God. We call it the law."

As my whole class tried to soak up this graceful and challenging message, the rabbi summed up by saying, "For any good Jew, the law is a sign of God's grace and love. It has nothing to do with earning salvation. In fact, it has been my perception that it is you Christians who are always trying to find ways to earn your salvation. You've got to believe this or do that before you can be sure God loves you. Earning salvation through some kind of works of the law has always been a Christian problem, not a Jewish one."

If we read Paul's letter to the Galatians with the knowledge of who he was writing to, we know this is true. Paul was writing to non-Jews. These non-Jews became convinced that they had to follow Jewish law, keep kosher, and be circumcised before they could be sure God loved them. They worried about whether they were doing what was right and good to earn God's love. It was non-Jews, Gentile Christians, who were obsessed with preconditions for grace.

As I argue in the previous chapter, the same is true today. In the contemporary public definition of Christianity, we are obsessed with believing the right things, or with having enough faith, to earn God's love and salvation. Trying to earn salvation has always been a Christian obsession. Instead of realizing that fact, we have often projected it onto our mistaken view of Judaism. We should remember Paul's message to the non-Jews of Galatia, for it is a message applicable to Gentiles today. Paul entrusted to the Galatians, and to us, the message that our salvation is a gift bestowed upon on us by the faithfulness of Jesus, the Christ, and not because of anything we have done or anything we have believed.

Unfortunately, we still don't hear this message. Like the Galatians of old, we come up with all kinds of prerequisites for God's love and salvation. But if we take the letter to Galatians seriously and read it in conjunction with all of the letters of Paul, we can have confidence in the incredible love of God as revealed in the faith *of* Jesus Christ. Jesus proclaimed the love of God even when he was rejected on the cross. Such a love freely offered can never be defeated—and neither can it be earned. It simply is. And it is ours to be received as a gift from a loving and generous God.

CHAPTER 8

⚮

LIVING BY THE GRACE OF GOD

The man was distraught. He had done something of which he was ashamed, and now he was trying to pick up the pieces of his life and make amends to those he'd harmed. He was in my office to ask how he could ever walk back into church again. How could he ever face God, or me, a minister, after admitting to this failure?

"What must you think of me?" he asked.

"I don't think any less of you now than I did before you told me all this," I said.

A look of surprise crossed his face. "But how?"

"God loves you," I said, "and so do I. You're an imperfect human being, just like me. If we had to be perfect before God could love us then we would never be loved. The fact that you're making amends is a good thing. I can't take away the consequences of your actions, but I can assure you of God's love and forgiveness."

This is just one story from among dozens from my life as an ordained minister. It is an encounter that repeats itself on a regular basis. And each time it does I've found that it is the love of God that leads people beyond despondency. Guilt, self-flagellation, and fear of God's wrath and judgment are terrible motivators for change—they're more likely to inspire depression and self-hatred.

Most people, I've found, tend to view God as a great traffic cop in the sky, keeping track of all our rights and wrongs. When we're good, God approves of us, and we expect to be rewarded with a good, pain-free, or easy life. And when we're bad, God disapproves and is ready to punish us for our sins, by sending us misfortune, illness, or problems in this life and, of course, damning us to hell in the next. This is hardly a view fitting with the God described by Saint Paul and in the Gospels.

Sometimes we can't see the love of God until we experience failure or sinfulness, and someone reminds us that even in the midst of it all we're still loved by God. I know that was the case for me. There was a time in my life when I made some poor choices that put my primary relationships in jeopardy. In addition, my job prospects were grim. I felt as if everything of importance in my life was in doubt. And I asked myself, "Is there anything I can be sure of?"

Thank God I grew up in a household, and in a church, that constantly reminded me of the love of God. In that time of desperation and fear, it suddenly dawned on me that the one thing I couldn't doubt was that God loved me. Assured of that reality, my life began to change. I had the courage to make amends for my failures. I had the strength to reinvest in my relationships. I found the resolve to seek education that opened up new opportunities for employment.

When we begin with God's love, rather than with God as the traffic cop in the sky, amazing things can happen. We have already been saved by the faith of Jesus Christ. While we were stuck in our sins and problems, Christ died for us. God loves us no matter what. It is this reality that can bring us beyond guilt and shame and can transform us into new people.

But transforming us beyond our crises and failures is not the only thing the love of God can do for us. It can also open up new understandings that help bring us life-giving joy. I will always remember the time I saw this happen to a woman in one of the churches I've served.

"Kate" was agitated. She had only been visiting the church for a few weeks.

"I'm not sure why I'm here," she said. "I'm spiritual but not religious. In fact, I have a real problem with the institutional Church. It's obsessed with its own survival, and it often protects abusive leaders. But I need community. I need a place to help me understand my relationship with God, but I'm afraid."

"Afraid of what?" I asked.

"Well, I'm afraid that if I come here to church then you're going to tell me I have to believe in things that I just find ludicrous."

"Like what?" I asked.

"Like the virgin birth. I have a real problem with that. Why do I have to believe something I find absurd, that God would break God's own laws for the way reproduction works. Why do I have to believe such a thing in order to be saved, or to be a Christian?"

"You don't have to believe it to be saved," I said. And then I went on to explain how I believe God's love and salvation are gifts that don't depend on us or on anything we do or believe. I also went on to tell her that believing in the literal fact of the virgin birth is not the point of our saying in the Creed that we believe Jesus was born of the Virgin Mary. Believing in the virgin birth isn't about believing God can break God's own laws if God chooses to do so. If God wants to do that, I am sure God can, but that is beside the point. The virgin birth is a means of expressing a truth beyond fact. And that truth is that we believe Jesus was not only a human being but that he also revealed the fullness of God. To proclaim that reality, we say that God's initiative (the virgin birth) was integral to Jesus' existence. In essence, the virgin birth tells us that God was choosing to be revealed in Jesus of Nazareth. But Mary plays an important role, too. She says yes. Mary's assent reminds us that God's initiative can do very little if we human beings don't respond to it. These are the things the virgin birth tells us: that God chooses, by God's own initiative, to be revealed to us, and that we can avail ourselves of that reality when we say yes to God. That, after all, is a belief that matters much more than believing God can break the rules of science and reproduction. It is also a belief that has an impact on our lives. We can believe God takes the initiative to seek us out and to love us. We can believe that our response to this initiative matters, and that by responding to God something new can be revealed in our lives that proclaims the presence of God in the here and now. I asked "Kate" if she believed the things I just described about God's love and initiative and our response to it.

"Of course," she said.

"Then I would say you believe in the virgin birth."

Surprised by this answer, "Kate" began to ask me about the creation, miracles, and a host of other accounts from our Christian tradition that made her nervous. As a modern woman, she just couldn't buy into reading the Bible as if it were a history text or a science book. She felt an incredible freedom when I told her she didn't have to—that although God can do anything God wants, the point of the miracles and creation stories isn't to prove an alternate scientific reality that God is in charge of. No, there are truths behind each of these accounts that are much bigger than the mere description of events. Creation tells us of our origin in and dependence on God for existence. Miracles tell us that personal transformation—a miracle in itself—is possible.

"Believing things you find absurd is not what salvation is all about," I told her. "Salvation is about responding to a God who loves you and desires what is best for you, which you already seem to be doing by coming here and seeking community."

"Kate" came to church regularly after that and found strength for her spiritual journey and growth in her life of faith.

This story, too, is a composite. It has been repeated over and over with men, women, and young people. The fact that this encounter keeps repeating itself is a result of the public definition of Christianity. People who reject the current popular definition of the faith are sometimes reluctant to associate with any church.

"So if grace is completely free," you may still be asking, "do I have to believe anything or do anything?" This is the question I always get asked when I proclaim the incredible gift of God's love as a given, available without preconditions. And I always answer the same way: "No. You don't have to do anything or believe anything to be loved by God. However, if you want to get the greatest benefit from that love, then yes—there are things to believe and do."

WHY SOME BELIEFS AND BEHAVIORS HELP

The love of God would do us very little good if we didn't believe God even existed. The love of God would do us very little good if we believed that all we needed to get along in life was ourselves and those closest to us and nothing else, not even God. The love of God would do us very little good if we had no witnesses to the power of that love in the lives of others as revealed in scripture, the Creeds, the history of the Church, and even the present Church community. The love of God would do us very little good if we had no expectations for how we share that love with others and model it in our own lives and with our own behavior. Yes, beliefs help, morals help, and actions help. I only argue that they are not prerequisites for salvation. Instead, they become means by which we access the joy of living into that salvation, living by the grace of God.

If we acknowledge there is a God and that God loves us, then we can be open to the idea that our lives will be enriched by God's love. If we read the scriptures and the Church's history, we can benefit from the example of others who have known the love of God. If we participate in a church community, we can experience the love of God in worship, pastoral care, and fellowship. And if we live a moral life, we can model the love of God to the world around us. None of these things are preconditions for receiving God's love. Instead, they represent ways that God helps us benefit most from the love he already gives.

Let me offer some examples from my previous descriptions of the terms *belief, religion*, and *faith*. First, we believe in a God who loves us. That in itself is a rather audacious claim. Christianity dares to declare that the one who created this vast universe, with millions of galaxies and billions of stars, actually loves each and every one of us. Then, once we accept such a belief, we can practice a religion based on God's love. We are worthy of God's love, and so is everyone else, along with all of creation. We live a moral life in order to treat others and the world around us—and ourselves—with the same love we believe God holds for each of us. That is our religion. In fact, such things are at the heart of all religious teaching and doctrine: Live as if God loved you, everyone else, and all of creation. Then, finally, we have a faithful relationship with the creator of the universe, as revealed in the life, death, and resurrection of Jesus the Christ, in the biblical witness of our ancestors in the faith, in the Creeds and history of the Church, and in a spiritual life nourished by prayer. Yes, beliefs, morals, and faith, though they are not preconditions to God's love, do help us to experience it. And when we experience the love of God, we in essence open the doorway into experiencing eternal life in the here and now, just as John's gospel said we would.

WHAT ABOUT HEAVEN?

Once I begin to describe, in classes or sermons, this idea of believing and acting in ways that allow the love of God to be for our benefit in the here and now, then someone always asks, "What about heaven? You're talking only about this life. Don't you believe in heaven?" If the people asking this question know their Bible, they often cite 1 Corinthians 15:19: "If for this life only we have hoped in Christ, we are of all people most to be pitied."

Yes, I believe in heaven. The older I get, and the more I lose loved ones to death, the more strongly I hope and believe. But let me rephrase Paul's admonition about our hope of heaven in this way: If there is no evidence in this life giving us glimpses of the life to come, then we indeed should be pitied.

But just as the notion of salvation pertains not only to the next life, so I believe the concept of heaven isn't just about the next life. We are afforded glimpses of it here. In fact, I often say that living a life of faith, a life infused with the love of God, is not about earning our way into heaven, but rather about helping us see if we're going to like it when we get there. If heaven is like the kingdom of God Jesus described, then the last will be first, the stranger will be welcomed, the little child will lead us, we will serve one another, the sinner will be forgiven, and we will all forgive one another. If we can't live that way now, will we even like it when we arrive in the hereafter? But if we are already trying to live by Jesus' description of the kingdom, not only will this life be richer, but it will offer glimpses of the life to come.

These thoughts have influenced the way I prepare for funerals. In my tradition, that of the Episcopal Church, eulogies are frowned upon. This comes from our belief in grace as a free gift. A eulogy, with all its high praise for the deceased, often comes across as an argument for why this person deserves to go to heaven, or why they have earned their own salvation. Since we don't want to send such a works righteousness message about the life to come, we Episcopalians avoid eulogies.

But dealing with grief demands some mention of the life of the deceased, some means of setting that person's life in the context of faith and hope, even in the midst of tears. I've found a way to do this with funeral sermons that stays true to my belief that we see glimpses of the life to come in the here and now.

My funeral sermons always point out that we gather at a funeral not only to mourn the deceased, but to proclaim our hope of heaven and a life to come where we all will be together again. Then I say that the best place to look for this hope is in the best things about the deceased's life. It is there, in moments of selfless love and commitment, in efforts to make the world a better place for all those around them, that we get glimpses of our hope. In the here and now, we have touched heaven in those events that bring out the best in us. We didn't earn these glimpses of heaven, but witnessed them as a gift in the life of the beloved deceased.

PROCLAIMING THE GOOD NEWS

To say that God loves us, no matter what, is good news. To say that God will love us when we properly accept that love through some kind of ritualized prayer, or when we believe all the right things about God, or behave according to a very strict set of morals, is something else. I don't know what that is, but it certainly doesn't sound like good news.

There are three ways for us to share this good news of God's love. First, we can live it. We can be thankful for the love of God. We can enjoy our lives, the creation in which we find ourselves, and the love for and with others that gives us glimpses into the fullness of God's love. We can allow that love to bring us through the crises in our lives. We can allow that love to transform us when we've failed or need to make a change. We can allow that love to lead us in ethical and moral behavior, not as a way of avoiding hell, but as a way of living life to the fullest with respect for the world around us.

Second, we can invite others into that love. I have no problem inviting people to church. I enjoy doing so. I love my church and want to share its message of God's love with others. In that sense, I consider myself an evangelical. But people are often suspicious of my invitations, because of the current public face of Christianity. They seem nervous and edgy when I talk to them about coming to church. Some have told me they are afraid I'll start telling them they'll go to hell if they don't come or if they don't believe in the right things. I respond that I know God loves them already. I'm inviting them to church not to earn that love but to experience it. Unfortunately, in many of their previous encounters with church people, they haven't experienced much love at all, and so they're wary. In the end, I may invite people, but I don't feel I've failed or consigned them to hell if they don't respond. That's not the kind of God I believe in. I don't think that's the kind of God Jesus told us about.

One of the best ways we can share the good news is by striving for God's kingdom. We can work for the values Jesus proclaimed in his kingdom parables, by seeking the lost, caring for the least, honoring the humble, forgiving one another, feeding the hungry, visiting the sick, and doing the many, many things Jesus challenged us to do as a way of sharing his love. We have learned from history that we can't fully create the kingdom of God on earth. But that doesn't absolve us from working for it as best we can.

I remember two examples of seeking the kingdom from my own life that have filled me with great joy. The first comes from an experience of forgiveness, not just receiving but extending it. When Jesus told parables about the kingdom, he often told ones about how we should forgive as we have been forgiven. For example, in the story of the unforgiving servant (Matthew 18:23–35), a man is forgiven a great debt by his king, yet when confronted with a lesser servant who owes him very little, he puts him in jail. Clearly, Jesus holds up this parable as a poor example of being a part of his kingdom. God forgives us; we are encouraged to forgive one another.

I learned this the hard way. At one point in my life, I carried a huge grudge against a fellow priest who had spread rumors about me and defamed me in the congregation I served. The rumors only died down with time, and some parishioners still believed them even years afterward. I was bitter and angry, and in prayer and reflection on the gospel, it suddenly dawned on me that I was the only person being hurt by this bitterness and anger. It was eating me up inside—not the person with whom I was angry. I realized that if I were to experience the fullness of God's love for me, then I had to let go of this anger and forgive my fellow priest. I wrote a letter offering forgiveness and asking this priest to forgive me for any wrongs I might have done. I never heard back, but from that point on I was released from my bitterness and anger in ways I couldn't have anticipated.

What made the story even more dramatic for me personally was that within a month after writing the letter, my bishop gave a huge gift to the church I served. It was the year 2000, and as a way of proclaiming a year of God's Jubilee, he forgave the $50,000 debt my congregation owed our diocese for the church building we had recently erected.

The next week, a photographer and reporter showed up from the local newspaper to do a story on me, the parish, and our forgiven debt. A few days later, my picture filled the entire top half of the front page of the Metro section, with a headline underneath that read, "Practicing Forgiveness." Little did the reporter (nor those who read the article) know that the headline was true in more ways than one. I'd practiced forgiveness not just by experiencing the forgiveness of a loan, but by letting go of a grudge against a fellow priest. By practicing the kingdom values of Jesus, I was set free and given new life.

The forgiveness of our congregation's debt led to another glimpse of Jesus' kingdom. Since our forgiven debt freed up money in our church's budget, our bishop encouraged us to use that money for a project that promoted God's kingdom. We debated for many months on what to do and finally settled on creating a program at four of our sister churches in the inner city.

We were a suburban church with very little contact with the inner city, but we knew that many of the Episcopal churches in the local city were in decline. They had lost touch with the poor neighborhoods around them. So we proposed a once-a-month Saturday morning program for the children who lived in the neighborhoods around these churches. The program would include worship, teaching, crafts, recreation, and food. It would offer Christian education to children who might not be receiving it. And through the children we would make the community aware of the church's presence and desire to serve the neighborhood. The inner-city congregations would provide the space and some volunteer coordination for the program. We would provide funding and as many volunteers as possible.

In all honesty, the program had mixed results. But in at least two congregations, the community's awareness of the local church was restored. Local neighborhood people, led by their children, began to attend. That in itself was a great success.

But what filled me with the greatest joy was watching the interaction between members of the suburban congregation I served and inner-city children. Women and men with expensive clothing and fancy jewelry on their hands were helping children from homes very different from their own, doing such simple things as teaching craft projects and working in the kitchen making cookies. Business owners stepped into the lives of young people whose parents were out of work. And after months of working together, these two groups of people began to greet each other by name and began to delight in one another's presence. People were transformed, and not just those in the inner-city neighborhoods. In the midst of this program, a countywide tax to improve inner-city schools appeared on the ballot, and many of the suburbanites volunteering in these local churches voted to support the tax because they knew children whose lives would be improved by it. Attitudes were changed. Prejudices melted away. Churches were restored to relationship with their surrounding communities. If that is not a glimpse of the kingdom of God, then I don't know what is.

SALVATION BEGINS AND ENDS WITH GOD'S LOVE

In the last twenty-five years, the public definition of Christianity has changed. Conservative evangelicals and fundamentalists now influence the dominant view. Many proclaim a message that is harsh, promotes conflict with other Christians, and offends others. Messages like "Convert or burn in hell" are popular. At the very least, modern Christianity seems obsessed with proclaiming a message that we should believe a certain set of narrow doctrines, or follow a restrictive set of morals, or have a particular kind of verifiable conversion experience, in order to make sure "our ticket is punched on the train to the afterlife."

This is not the only version of Christianity proclaimed in scripture or the history of the Church. Though I acknowledge views other than my own as one version of Christianity, I do not consider them the only legitimate version. In fact, I believe that anyone who claims as much is simply wrong.

The view of salvation I grew up with, and the one I have experienced in my life, begins with God's love. God loves us—no ifs, ands, or buts about it. And it is this love that can lead us to deeper beliefs in and about God. It is this love that can transform us and lead us away from immoral or self-destructive behavior. It is this love that can lead us to work for God's kingdom right here and right now. And it is this love that can reveal to all, in the here and now, glimpses of the heaven to come. That is our saving grace and salvation.

NOTES

1. Jeremy Rifkin and Ted Howard, *The Emerging Order: God in the Age of Scarcity* (New York: G. P. Putnam's Sons, 1979). Where Rifkin and Howard got it wrong was in thinking that the growing conservative movement in Christianity would embrace a theology that no longer valued wealth and consumption.

2. Marcus Borg and N. T. Wright, *The Meaning of Jesus: Two Views* (San Francisco: HarperCollins, 1999). The beauty of this book is that it was written by a conservative scholar (Wright) and a liberal one (Borg). Even though they did not agree on all of the historical conclusions, they were almost identical in their views about the Christian life: that it should be characterized by prayer and concern for improving the world around us.

3. Marcus Borg, *The God We Never Knew* (San Francisco: Harper-Collins, 1997), 18–19.

4. Bernard Anderson, *Understanding the Old Testament* (Edgewood Cliffs, New Jersey: Prentice-Hall, 1975), 8–10; and Brevard Childs, *The Book of Exodus* (Philadelphia: Westminster Press, 1974), 240–53.

5. Edward Schillebecckx, *Christ: The Experience of Jesus as Lord* (New York: Crossroads, 1977), 477–544.

6. C. H. Dodd, *The Interpretation of the Fourth Gospel* (Cambridge, MA: Cambridge University Press, 1953), 144–50.

7. *Lesser Feasts and Fasts* (New York: Church Hymnal Corporation, 1988), 161.

8. Edmund S. Morgan, *The Puritan Dilemma: The Story of John Winthrop* (Boston: Little, Brown and Company, 1958), 70.

9. George Forell, ed., *Christian Social Teaching* (Minneapolis: Augsburg, 1971), 371.

10. Ibid., 379.

11. Raymond Brown, *The Churches the Apostles Left Behind* (Mahwah, NJ: Paulist Press, 1984).

12. Adolph Spaeth, et al., trans. and eds., *Works of Martin Luther* (Philadelphia: A. J. Holman Company, 1915), vol. 1, 29–38. The actual text reads, in English, "Why does not the pope empty purgatory, for the sake of holy love and of the dire need of the souls that are there, if he redeems an infinite number of souls for the sake of miserable money with which to build a Church? The former reasons would be most just; the latter is most trivial" (Thesis 82).

13. Lloyd Gaston, *Paul and the Torah* (Vancouver: University of British Columbia Press, 1987), 103; and Raymond Brown, *An Introduction to the New Testament* (New York: Doubleday, 1997), 477–78.

14. Norman Perrin and Dennis C. Duling, *The New Testament: An Introduction* (New York: Harcourt, Brace Jovanovich, 1982), 35.